Joseph Le Roy Harrison

With Pipe and Book

A Collection of College Verse

Joseph Le Roy Harrison

With Pipe and Book
A Collection of College Verse

ISBN/EAN: 9783337217556

Printed in Europe, USA, Canada, Australia, Japan

Cover: Foto ©Thomas Meinert / pixelio.de

More available books at **www.hansebooks.com**

With Pipe and Book

A Collection of
... College Verse

Chosen by

Joseph Le Roy Harrison

Editor of " Cap and Gown "

"The philosophy of life's afternoon is a poor exchange for the poetry of its morning"

C. T. WINCHESTER

Preston and Rounds Company

Providence . . . M<small>DCCCXCVII</small>

Copyright, 1897,
By Preston and Rounds Company.

To

Col. Timothy Shaler Williams

COLLEGE PAPERS REPRESENTED

Amherst College . . .	Amherst Literary Monthly.
	Amherst Student.
Boston College	Stylus.
Brown University . . .	Brown Magazine.
	Brunonian.
Columbia University .	. Columbia Literary Monthly.
Cornell University . . .	Cornell Era.
	Cornell Magazine.
Dartmouth College .	. Dartmouth Literary Monthly.
Hamilton College . . .	Hamilton Literary Monthly.
Harvard University .	. Harvard Advocate.
Lehigh University . . .	Lehigh Burr.
Leland Stanford Jr. Univ. .	Sequoia.
Mount Holyoke College	. Mount Holyoke.
Notre Dame University	. Notre Dame Scholastic.
Princeton University .	. Nassau Literary Monthly.
	Princeton Tiger.
Smith College	. Smith College Monthly.
Trinity College	. Trinity Tablet.
University of Chicago .	. University of Chicago Weekly.
University of Michigan	. Inlander.
University of Minnesota	. Minnesota Magazine.
University of Pennsylvania.	Red and Blue.

College Papers Represented

University of Rochester	Campus.
University of Tennessee	Tennessee Univ. Magazine.
University of Vermont	University Cynic.
University of Virginia	Univ. of Virginia Magazine.
University of Wisconsin	Wisconsin Ægis.
Vassar College	Vassar Miscellany.
Washington and Lee Univ.	Southern Collegian.
Wellesley College	Wellesley Magazine.
Wesleyan University	Wesleyan Literary Monthly.
Williams College	Williams Athenæum.
	Williams Literary Monthly.
Yale University	Yale Courant.
	Yale Literary Magazine.
	Yale Record.

CONTENTS

April	Yale Literary Magazine, 52
At Sweet Sixteen . .	Tennessee Univ. Magazine, 52
At the Sea	Red and Blue, 115
Ballade of a Kiss, The .	Harvard Advocate, 113
Ballad of Dorothy, A .	Williams Literary Monthly, 36
Banquet Song . . .	Dartmouth Literary Monthly, 144
Bashful Johnny . .	Williams Literary Monthly, 33
Boccherini's Minuet .	Williams Athenæum, 40
Carpe Diem . . .	Univ. of Chicago Weekly, 2
Cheer	Brown Magazine, 120
Chivalry	Yale Literary Magazine, 62
Christmas Morning .	Yale Courant, 117
Cloudland	Columbia Literary Monthly, 136
Colin's Call . . .	Red and Blue, 44
Comin' thro' the Rye .	Yale Record, 30
Coquette, A . . .	Brunonian, 15
Crocuses, The . . .	Wellesley Magazine, 71
"Crux Fidelis" . .	Harvard Advocate, 135
Die Weinstube . . .	Yale Courant, 56
Di's Smile	Amherst Student, 139
Doris's Shoestrings . .	Vassar Miscellany, 146
Dorothy	Yale Courant, 58
Dream Song . . .	Smith College Monthly, 94
Drinking Song . . .	Brown Magazine, 24
Fairyland	Wellesley Magazine, 59
Fayre Ladye Lalage .	Harvard Advocate, 103
First Snowstorm, The .	Vassar Miscellany, 78

Contents

Free	Nassau Literary Monthly, 19
Free Lances . . .	Harvard Advocate, 67
Fool's Ballad . . .	Yale Courant, 145
Glee Club Concert, The.	Univ. of Chicago Weekly, 66
Heliotrope	Harvard Advocate, 108
Her Light Guitar . .	Amherst Literary Monthly, 148
Humble Romance, A .	Vassar Miscellany, 53
I Dream of Thee . .	Univ. of Chicago Weekly, 109
If I but knew . . .	Stylus, 55
Immer Mehr . . .	Harvard Advocate, 88
In Cap and Bells . .	Harvard Advocate, 105
Influence	Southern Collegian, 20
In Modern Times . .	Amherst Literary Monthly, 107
In the Dark . . .	Williams Literary Monthly, 61
In the Jim Valley . .	Minnesota Magazine, 41
In the Pines . . .	Vassar Miscellany, 18
Jacqueminot . . .	Wesleyan Literary Monthly, 99
Jock and Jenny . .	Yale Courant, 76
Late	Wisconsin Ægis, 119
Letting down the Bars .	Red and Blue, 101
Lines	Cornell Era, 129
Little Bird, A . . .	Smith College Monthly, 22
Little Blind Beggar, The .	Smith College Monthly, 128
"Little Dan Cupid " .	Vassar Miscellany, 25
Lost Love	Lehigh Burr, 92
Love's Origin . . .	Brunonian, 70
Lullaby	Wellesley Magazine, 34
Lullaby	Wellesley Magazine, 86
Mabel	Red and Blue, 65
Manoa	Brown Magazine, 126
May Song, A . . .	Univ. of Chicago Weekly, 98
Midsummer Night's Dream, A . . .	Mount Holyoke, 131
Misunderstanding, A .	Wellesley Magazine, 69

Contents

Month of Magic, The .	Wesleyan Literary Monthly, 23
My Hounds	Vassar Miscellany, 89
My Lady in the Garden.	Dartmouth Literary Monthly, 125
My Lady Nicotine . .	Columbia Literary Monthly, 84
My Old Guitar . .	Yale Record, 75
My Pipe	Lehigh Burr, 48
My Quest	Trinity Tablet, 114
Night Wind's Song, The .	Inlander, 85
Nineteenth Century, The .	Williams Literary Monthly, 64
Now and Then . .	Trinity Tablet, 106
Oh, for the storm-scarred headlands . .	Harvard Advocate, 51
Old Love Song, The .	Campus, 137
On the Retired List .	Princeton Tiger, 38
Polly, my Sweetheart .	Inlander, 72
"Poor Cupid froze his wings one day " .	Wellesley Magazine, 39
Prom. Roses . . .	Yale Record, 91
Ring-doves and Roses .	Yale Courant, 50
Rondeau	Smith College Monthly, 68
Rondeau : With Pipe and Book . . .	Yale Courant, 13
Saint Nicholas — His Roundelay . . .	Yale Courant, 28
Serenade	Williams Literary Monthly, 112
Since Agnes died . .	Brown Magazine, 27
Skating Song, A . .	Nassau Literary Monthly, 121
Slumber Song . . .	University Cynic, 131
Song	Red and Blue, 101
Song	Williams Literary Monthly, 73
Song, A	Nassau Literary Monthly, 134
Song of Joy, A . .	Univ. of Chicago Weekly, 14
Song of Mistress Anne, A .	Williams Literary Monthly, 17
Song of Return . .	Univ. of Chicago Weekly, 90
Song of the Jolly Fat Friar, The . . .	Harvard Advocate, 80

Contents

Song of the Sea Flight . Amherst Literary Monthly, 97
So runs the World . . Vassar Miscellany, 35
Southern . . . . Cornell Era, 148
Star of Bethlehem, The . Vassar Miscellany, 93
Stolen Glance, A . . Brunonian, 139
Suppose . . . . . Wellesley Magazine, 80
Sword Song . . . Hamilton Literary Monthly, 109

Tardy-bug Men, The . Minnesota Magazine, 141
Three Points of View . Notre Dame Scholastic, 123
To a Friend in Love . Wesleyan Argus, 47
To a Girl on a Greek
   Frieze . . . . Wesleyan Argus, 46
To a Miniature . . Vassar Miscellany, 21
To a Spray of Violets . Red and Blue, 104
To the Valley of Dreams. Notre Dame Scholastic, 150
Triolet . . . . . Sequoia, 60
Twilight Song . . . Vassar Miscellany, 63
Twilight Song . . . Yale Courant, 118

Upon her Mandolin . Harvard Advocate, 78

Valentine, A . . . Williams Literary Monthly, 82

When chime the Bells. Brunonian, 143
When Love was born . Cornell Era, 83
When Morning breaks. Cornell Magazine, 140
When Stars come out . Univ. of Virginia Magazine, 124
"When the last light,
   dim and still " . . Yale Literary Magazine, 133
When the Tide is low . University Cynic, 111
Where Cupid dwells . Yale Courant, 95
Where Love dwells . Yale Courant, 87
With Jenny in the Rain. Yale Courant, 45
Woodland Whispers . Univ. of Virginia Magazine, 96

Ye Golde-headed Cane. Wesleyan Literary Monthly, 31
Yesterday . . . . Southern Collegian, 119

With Pipe and Book

RONDEAU

WITH pipe and book, an old arm-chair,
    A glowing hearth, what need I care
For empty honors, wealth or fame?
Grant me but this; an honest name,
A cup of ale, a coat to wear.
And then, while smoke-wreaths rift the air,
The banquet of the gods I share,
Content to sit before the flame
    With pipe and book.

Above the city's noisy glare,
Yet sweet, tho' humble, is my fare.;
    For changing not from praise to blame,
    These faithful friends are still the same —
No earthly comforts can compare
    With pipe and book.

CHARLES E. MERRILL, JR.

A SONG OF JOY

I

Sing songs of gladness
  Merry and gay,
Mad with the madness
  Of life's roundelay;
Lays turned to lightness
  Sweet as the day,
Full of the brightness
  Of love's holiday.

II

Sing songs of gladness
  Joyous and free,
Scatter life's sadness
  Mid jollity;
Make music's measure
  Rolic and ring,
Pent with the pleasure
  Of youth and the spring.

III

Sing songs of gladness
  Merry with mirth,

… Laugh away sadness,
   Gladden the earth;
Burst out in singing,
   Sing all the day, —
'Ere life may be bringing
   Death to thy play.

CHARLES SUMNER PIKE.

A COQUETTE

OH, I see where you're sitting,
Out there with your knitting;
You thought you were hid by the trunk of the tree.
But, Kitty, believe me,
You cannot deceive me,
I'd find you wherever you happened to be.

CHORUS:

  Then 'tis come to me, Kitty,
  It's you that looks pretty,
  With your neat little feet and your trim little waist.

With Pipe and Book

So don't be so simple,
But bring me that dimple,
And give your own Barney a bit of a taste.

How your needles are flying,
As with them you're tying
And looping away at your bright worsted thread;
And it's little you're caring
If in it you're snaring
The heart of a lover you never would wed.

CHORUS:

   Then it's come to me, Kitty, etc.

Though your fingers are dancing,
I see that your're glancing
Aside at me here through the tail of your eye.
Then why should you wait, now,
But come to the gate, now,
And give me a kiss while I bid you good-bye.

CHORUS:

   Then it's come to me, Kitty, etc.

HENRY MORGAN STONE.

A SONG OF MISTRESS ANNE

In farthingale and satin gown,
      Sing hey, my lady !
Comes Mistress Anne from London-town
To Dingledale on Crosswood Down
      When country lanes are shady !

Blue are her eyes as June-tide skies,
      Sing hey, my lady !
June's sunshine in her soft hair lies,
Oh, who will win her beauty's prize
      When country lanes are shady ?

She lays aside her satin gown,
      Sing hey, my lady !
And dons a frock o' russet brown,
To pluck dog-roses on the Down
      When country lanes are shady!

O rustic swains, who find her fair,
      Sing hey, my lady !
Trust not her simple artless air,
Unless, perchance, she flout you there
      Where country lanes are shady !

ARTHUR KETCHUM.

IN THE PINES

There were three of us — Cupid went with us, you know,
Dear blindfolded boy, who is never *de trop*,
And the words left unsaid the soft winds whispered low,
      In the pines.

A small gift she gave me — though blind, it is true,
From the way that he laughed I am sure Cupid knew,
And the asters and goldenrod, they saw it too,
      And the pines.

Then the shadows grew dark in the wood's tangled growth,
And homeward we turned in the twilight, half loath,
And Love walked between with an arm around both,
      Through the pines.

                    JULIET WILBUR TOMPKINS.

A Collection of College Verse

FREE

Loosed are the bonds that held my soul,
   And afar on the leaping bay
I steer with the North Star for my goal,
   At the close of the autumn day.
      Then hey! for the rush of the cutting prow
         And the thrill of a wild delight —
      Where the bell-buoy swings as the sea-gull clings
         I gloom thro' the wave-born night.

I was clamped by a horror beyond all name,
   A plaything to bless or to ban,
Till the spirit within me surged in flame
   And I knew I was yet a man.
      Then hey! for the great brown wing I love,
         The swoop of the sail in the breeze,
      For the jarring sound of the past is drowned
         'Mid the clash of the tumbling seas.

The will has won in a life's revolt —
   A weird voice bids me forth —

With Pipe and Book

And keen as the stabbing thunderbolt
  I haste toward the mystic north.
      Then hey! for the whirlwind, headlong, grim,
        And hey! for the ice-king's glee.
  Thro' zephyr and gale alike I sail —
    Unfettered and fierce and free.

DAVID POTTER.

INFLUENCE

I wonder if ever a wave ebbs out but it breaks on a distant shore,
    Or fall any tears
    But the faces of years
Are stained thro' the Evermore?

I wonder if ever a day is born or an evening to twilight steals,
    But they leave a mark
    Thro' the gathering dark
In the print of their golden wheels?

A Collection of College Verse

I wonder if ever a word is said or ever a song
    is sung,
        But their souls live on
        When their sounds are gone —
In the Palace of Silence hung?

I wonder if ever a life is lived but its being gives
    sweet to some,
        But its hands touch still,
        And its dream-voice will
Speak after its lips are dumb?

And so may it be, thou forgotten one, when
    the cup of thy life is filled,
        That the world drink up
        From the shattered cup
Whatever and all that is spilled.

                  WILLIAM H. FIELD.

TO A MINIATURE

Sweet maid of old, with powdered hair,
With face and form forever fair,
Such joy was never seen before;

With Pipe and Book

Thou'st smiled for fifty years and more.
Didst never weep nor feel a care?

Did lovers brave always adore,
And noble vows breathe o'er and o'er?
Such homage now indeed is rare,
   Sweet maid of old.

Art never weary sitting there
In the old-fashioned, high-back chair?
Tell me, dear maiden, I implore,
Did blessings ever on thee pour,
And was the whole world, like thee, fair,
   Sweet maid of old?

MARIE REIMER.

A LITTLE BIRD

A LITTLE bird in a tree
Made one — a man and maiden three.
'Twas not by chance that they had met!
"None see," they said; one can forget
          A little bird.

A Collection of College Verse

A long hot road, a strip of grass,
'Twould tempt the Fates to let it pass!
Two people linger in the walk;
There's only one to hear them talk,
                A little bird.

Long shadows stretched across the sky,
Two people parted with a sigh,
But there was no one there to see!
How do I know? and who told me?
                A little bird.

                        E. R. C.

THE MONTH OF MAGIC

WHEN the bee, that idle skipper,
   Steers his shallop down the breeze;
Launching from the lady's slipper,
   Anchoring in the lilac trees, —
When the marsh-bird's ditty amorous
   (Where the indian-turnip grows)
Mingles with the pæan clamorous
   From the black heart of the crows, —
When the breath of roses lingers
   Like an incense in the sky, —

With Pipe and Book

When the odor of syringas
    Tempts the vagrant butterfly, —
When the moth, a knavish fellow,
    Steals the coins of gold that shine
In the cowslip's purse of yellow,
    Sacks and robs the lily's shrine, —
When the ether throbs with question —
    Intimation — whispered prayer —
Orioles, full of sly suggestion,
    Drop a hint down through the air, —
Then by some strange necromancy
    Sad old Earth is set to tune ;
Would you know the cause ? *I* fancy
    Heaven is keeping tryst with June.

              FREDERIC LAWRENCE KNOWLES.

DRINKING SONG

Ring from the rim of the glass, boys,
    Ripples of tinkling tones.
Drink to the heyday of youth, boys,
    Mindless of after moans.

Over the rim of the glass, boys,
  Gaze into eyes that are bright.
Drink with each sip of the wine, boys,
  Passionate gleams of delight.

Sing to the rim of the glass, boys,
  Chorus wherever we roam.
Drink to the sparkling-eyed depths, boys,
  A love as light as its foam.

Kiss the rim of the glass, boys,
  Blind to its siren-gleam.
Drink to its shading depths, boys,
  The wav'ring forms of a dream.

Then ring from the rim of the glass, boys,
  Ripples of tinkling tones.
Drink to the heyday of youth, boys,
  Mindless of after-moans.

JOHN CLINTON ANTHONY.

"LITTLE DAN CUPID"

Little Dan Cupid stole down on a sunbeam,
  To get of this old earth a peep.

With Pipe and Book

He was tired of play with toy hearts and blunt arrows,
  And his good mother Love was asleep.

Little Dan Cupid rode home on the moon-ray,
  And bore to his mother as trophies of might
Two human hearts, pierced and bleeding, enfolded
  In a bit of the gray mist that shrouded the night.

"Ah, naughty Dan Cupid!" Love cried; her tears falling
  Were like the sweet dropping of soft April rain;
"Knewest thou not that in all the wide heaven
  No healing is found for Love's wounds or Love's pain?"

The pitying All-Mother took to her bosom
  The poor beating things by Dan Cupid undone.
"At least, ye may bear it together," she murmured,
  And tenderly kissed the two souls into one.

AMY LOUISE REED.

A Collection of College Verse

SINCE AGNES DIED

They say that the brook makes music soft
    As ever in its pebbly bed,
That the leaves still whisper sweet aloft
    In springtime when the robins wed.
Well, yes, they may — I cannot say —
      Since Agnes died.

They say the sunshine still is fair,
    That the summer air is still as sweet,
When soft the breeze sighs everywhere
    In autumn, ere the long days fleet.
Perhaps 'tis so — I do not know —
      Since Agnes died.

They say that gladness is not dead,
    That the future smiles, and life is gay,
That joy and hope have not all fled,
    That comfort has not passed away.
It may be — well — I cannot tell —
      Since Agnes died.

          ALBERT ELLSWORTH THOMAS.

SAINT NICHOLAS — HIS ROUNDELAY

   On Christmas eve
   You would scarce believe
How early the sand-man came a-creeping;
   By the way each head
   Went into the bed
   When prayers were said
You'd have thought them sleeping.
(You would really have thought the children sleeping.)
   Sing Fol-de-rol-dol-diddle-lol-day,
   Saint Nicholas — his roundelay.

   Old Saint Nick
   With his usual trick
Came upon the roof with a terrible clatter;
   And Dolly and Sue,
   And Polly and Prue,
   And Jonathan too,
Knew what was the matter.
(But of course they didn't wake up at the clatter.)
   Sing Fol-de-rol-dol-diddle-lol-day,
   Saint Nicholas — his roundelay.

A Collection of College Verse

   Little Miss Polly
   Dreamed of a dolly,
Hung by the wrist to a Christmas tree,
   And a candy boar,
   With an echoing roar,
   From the e-qua-tor
To the frozen sea.
(An astonishing boar, 'twixt you and me.)
    Sing Fol-de-rol-dol-diddle-lol-day,
    Saint Nicholas — his roundelay.

   Jonathan's fox
   And his Jack-in-the-box,
Would beat Sam Joneses all to nuthin'.
   Last Christmas he
   Had no monkey
   Made beautifully,
With sawdust stuffin.
(Oh, Sam Jones, he didn't 'mount to nuthin'.)
    Sing Fol-de-rol-dol-diddle-lol-day,
    Saint Nicholas — his roundelay.

   Ah, Christmas Day!
   The old folks say.
They sleep through the night and it doesn't matter;

With Pipe and Book

  For Dolly and Sue,
  And Polly and Prue,
  And Jonathan too,
Make up for the clatter
Of Nick in the night, that's the truth of the matter.
  Sing Fol-de-rol-dol-diddle-lol-day,
  Saint Nicholas — his roundelay.
       ROBERT L. MUNGER.

COMIN' THRO' THE RYE

 A DAINTY little maiden
  Came a-tripping through the rye,
An airy bit of womanhood,
  With laughter in her eye.
A jaunty little lassy,
  With a little coy way,
As merrily she tripped along
  To that natty Scottish lay:
  "*Gin a-body meet a-body*
    Comin' thro' the rye,
  Gin a-body kiss a-body
    Need a-body cry?"

A Collection of College Verse

A brawny, Scottish laddie
   Was a-working in the rye;
A brawny, fearless fellow,
   But a trifle bit too shy.
A bashful, blushing laddie,
   At that coy maiden's dare,
As merrily she tripped along
   To that natty Scottish air.

H. H. TOWNSEND.

YE GOLDE-HEADED CANE

It stands in the corner yet, stately and tall,
   With a top that once shone like the sun;
It whispers of musterfield, playhouse and ball,
   Of gallantries, courtship and fun.
It is hardly the stick for the dude of to-day,
   He would swear it was "deucedly plain,"
But the halos of memory crown its decay —
   My grandfather's gold-headed cane.

It could tell how a face in a circling calash
   Grew red as the poppies she wore,

With Pipe and Book

When a dandy stepped up with a swagger and
    dash
  And escorted her home to her door.
How the beaux cried with jealousy, "Jove!
    what a buck!"
  As they glared at the fortunate swain,
And the wand which appeared to have fetched
    him his luck —
  My grandfather's gold-headed cane.

It could tell of the rides in the grand yellow
    gig
  When, from under a broad scuttle hat,
The eyes of fair Polly were lustrous and big,
  And — but no! would it dare tell of *that*?
Ah me! by those wiles that bespoke the coquette
  How many a suitor was slain!
There was one though who conquered the foe
    when they met
  With the gleam of his gold-headed cane.

Oh the odors of lavender, lilac and musk!
  They scent these old halls even yet;
I can still see the dancers as down through the
    dusk
  They glide in the grave minuet.

A Collection of College Verse

The small satin slippers, my grandmamma's
    pride,
  Long, long in the chest have they lain;
Let us shake out the camphor and place them
    beside
  My grandfather's gold-headed cane.

FREDERIC LAWRENCE KNOWLES.

BASHFUL JOHNNY

Young bashful Johnny loved sweet May,
And went to court her every day,
But yet his tongue could never swear
  He loved her true.
It seems to me had I been there
  I'd vowed my love — now wouldn't you?

Sweet May would sit by Johnny's side,
And all her thoughts to him confide,
Yet take her hand he'd never dare —
  So near his, too —
It seems to me had I been there
  I'd clasped it tight — now wouldn't you?

With Pipe and Book

And May's red lips seemed to invite
Sweet kisses; but so bold a flight
He thought — yet wondered if she'd care —
  Would never do.
It seems to me had I been there
  I would have kissed her — wouldn't you?

GEORGE W. GILLETTE.

LULLABY

Breezes in the tree-tops high,
  Sighing softly as you blow,
Sing a restful lullaby;
  Sing the sweetest song you know,
    Something slow, something low, —
    Lulla-lullaby.

Barley heads and crested wheat,
  Swaying gently to and fro,
Sing the music of the heat,
  Sing the drowsiest song you know,
    Something slow, something low, —
    Lulla-lullaby.

A Collection of College Verse

Brooklet hidden in the grass,
   Murmuring faintly as you flow,
Sing a sleep song while you pass;
   Sing the dreamiest song you know,
     Something slow, something low, —
       Lulla-lullaby.

              EMILY S. JOHNSON.

SO RUNS THE WORLD

Many a day, many a day,
A stalwart knight on a charger gray
Galloped along the king's highway.
   Never he stopped at the garden gate,
   Never he looked through the iron grate,
   But ever he whispered, "'Tis late, 'tis late,
   I seek for my princess, I cannot wait."
   (So runs the world, my dear.)

Many a day, many a day,
In the garden close by the king's highway
A lady sat spinning her bridal array.
   Never she thought of the garden gate,
   Never she stopped to look through the grate,

With Pipe and Book

But ever she whispered, "'Tis late, 'tis late,
My prince is coming, I cannot wait."
   (So runs the world, my dear.)

The roses beckoned over the wall,
The roadside birds never ceased to call,
The winds in passing told it all, —
  "She is here, she is here;"
But the prince rode into the world away,
And the princess spun her bridal array,
Till youth was ended and life was gray.
   (So runs the world, my dear.)

FANNY L. McKINNEY.

A BALLAD OF DOROTHY

It's "Dorothy! where's Dorothy?"
  From morn to even fall,
There's not a lad on Cowslip Farm
  Who joins not in the call.
It's Dolly here and Dolly there,
  Where can the maiden be?
No wench in all our country-side's
  So fine as Dorothy.

A Collection of College Verse

With tucked-up gown and shining pail
  Before the day is bright,
Down dewy lanes she singing goes
  Among the hawthorns white.
Perchance, her roses need her care
  She tends them faithfully.
There's not a rose in all the world
  As fresh and sweet as she !

With morning sunshine in her hair
  A-churning Dolly stands.
Oh, happy churn ! I envy it,
  Held close between her hands ;
And when the crescent moon hangs bright
  Athwart the soft night sky,
Down shadowed paths we strolling go,
  Just Dorothy and I.

As true of heart, as sweet of face,
  With gay and girlish air,
The painted belles of citydom
  Are not a whit as fair.
Come Michaelmas the parish chimes
  Will ring out merrily.

With Pipe and Book

Who is the bride I lead to church?
Why, who but Dorothy?

ARTHUR KETCHUM.

ON THE RETIRED LIST

Vet'ran dress-coat! You've gone astray,
Yes, you, old soldier, worn and gray.
　But ah! High pride must have its falls;
　You will get tight; the habit galls,
So you're retired — laid away.
Yet you've faced powder, blithe and gay,
The "awful charge," the trumpet's bray;
　You've known the hum of whirling balls,
　　Vet'ran dress-coat.

Our fight is done. In deadly fray
We seized her heart. Though heroes lay
　Within the breach, we stormed the walls,
　And hung our banners in those halls;
By conquering "arms" we won the day,
　　Vet'ran dress-coat!

"POOR CUPID FROZE HIS WINGS ONE DAY"

Poor Cupid froze his wings one day,
When winds were cold and skies were gray,
   And clouds with snow were laden.
A little maid was passing by;
She caught the rogue,— he could not fly,—
   Oh naughty little maiden!

She sent him off with sharpen'd dart,
To steal for her a certain heart;
   But, oh the mishap stupid!
Since Cupid's blind, and cannot see,
He went astray, and came to me.
   Oh naughty little Cupid!

So that is why my heart is gone,
And I am dreary and forlorn,
   With tears my eyes are laden.
She does not want my heart — ah no!
I did not wish to have it go;
   Oh Cupid, and oh maiden!

GERTRUDE JONES.

With Pipe and Book

BOCCHERINI'S MINUET

Out upon the night air steals the music, soft and
    low,
Trembling like a wind-swayed leaflet swinging
    to and fro ;
    Ah, the whispered moaning,
    Ah, the soft intoning,
Ah, the dancers, buried long ago !

Louder grows the music now, and now a flick-
    ering glow
Shines upon the ghostly dancers, moving there
    below ;
    Ah, the courtly graces,
    Ah, the eager faces,
Of the dancers, buried long ago !

    How the jewels glisten,
        Diamonds, lustre-robbing !
    How the spectres listen
        To the music, sobbing !

O'er the waxen floor the bowing shadows
    slowly go ;

A Collection of College Verse

Then they vanish quickly, as the north wind
    drives the snow;
  Was it only seeming?
  Was I only dreaming
Of the dancers, buried long ago?

                    G. A. COPELAND.

IN THE JIM VALLEY

They're harvestin' the wheat-fields in the valley
    of the Jim;
I can hear the reapers clatter, soundin' kind of
    low and dim,
See the yello' fields a-wavin', an' the shocks in
    crooked rows,
An' the house an' barn, an' mother out hangin'
    up the clo'se;
See the cattle and the pastur', an' the ol' gray
    limpin' mule,
An' the yello' heifer standin' in the water
    keepin' cool;
An' I try to fight agin' it as a sort of silly whim,
But I wisht 'at I was back there in the valley
    of the Jim.

With Pipe and Book

Now it's fall; an' they're a thrashin' an' a
 ploughin' up the ground;
An' the air is sort of hazy, an' the gulls are
 sailin' 'round;
An' the sun looks kind of yello' in the smoky
 afternoon;
An' at evenin' you can listen to the thunder's
 sleepy tune,
See the horses comin' home from work, an'
 smell their sweaty coats,
Hear 'em smashin' through the stubble, tired
 an' hungry for their oats.
Now it's growing sort of dusky, an' they're
 doin' up the chores,
An' the kitchen fire is burnin', an' it's chilly
 out-o'-doors: —
I can smell the eggs an' coffee, an' I know my
 little trim,
Lovin' mother's gettin' supper in the valley by
 the Jim.

One't I had a older brother in the valley of the
 Jim;
An' he was a homely feller, an' I ust to go
 with him

A Collection of College Verse

To the pastur' for the cattle, an' a-fishin', an'
  around;
An' I mind he ust to carry me acrost the stubble
  ground,
An' we'd often sit a-fishin', on a summer after-
  noon,
By the creek, an' hear the gophers chirp, an'
  listen to the tune
Of the bob-o-link an' black-bird — oh I recol-
  lect it well;
An' we liked the sleepy water, an' the kind of
  fishy smell
Of the old dry bank, with craw-fish bones an'
  clam-shells layin' there;
An' we'd hear the dreary singin' of the plover
  in the air.
An' then one day in fall they buried him on
  father's hill;
'N I cried all day, an' wished 'at I was laid
  along of Bill;
Fer it seemed so queer an' lonesome 'thout no
  brother any more; —
An' now the grass is dyin' there, an' winds
  are sighin' o'er; —

With Pipe and Book

I can hear the sor'ful meado' lark a-singin' over him.—
O, I wisht 'at I was back there in the valley of the Jim.

WILL DILLMAN.

COLIN'S CALL

Oh! who will be my true love
 And put her hand in mine?
Oh! who will to the alleyed grove
 And garlands gay entwine?

For her who'll be my true love
 The fairest flowers I'll find;
The loveliest posies in the grove
 For her shall all be twined.

Oh! who'll be my true love
 And wander forth with me
To where the clouds float soft above,
 The primrose dots the lea?

For her who'll be my true love
 The skies will aye be blue,

A Collection of College Verse

The meadows always green prove,
   My heart be ever true.

F. T. W.

WITH JENNY IN THE RAIN

As sad I was as any,
   With all a lover's pain,
Till I walked that day with Jenny —
   With Jenny in the rain!
Past fresh'ning fields of clover
   And sweet with ripening grain,
And blossoms blowing over,
   With Jenny in the rain!

The silken shade above her —
   The violets at her feet;
The raindrops seemed to love her,
   And fell in music sweet.
And O, the south wind blowing
   In many a glad refrain,
When love and I were going
   With Jenny in the rain.

Each breeze that rippled past her
   Stole kisses on the way;

With Pipe and Book

The rain fell never faster
  Than beat my heart that day!
And O, the fields of clover,
  And O, the golden grain!
For love came home — the rover!
  With Jenny, in the rain!

FRANK L. STAMON.

TO A GIRL ON A GREEK FRIEZE

How often have I gazed into thy face,
And wished those lips could pulse again with red,
Those eyes could answer mine, thy feet could tread
The choral dance anew with old-time grace,
Thy rounded arms, which now entwine that vase,
And poise it high above that perfect head,
Could clasp me in their new-found warmth instead,
Thy heart could join with mine in sweet embrace.
Ah, then we'd leave the noisy, smoky town,

A Collection of College Verse

And through the fragrant meadows haste away
And whispering woods, to some fair sleepy
  glade,
Where fairies weave the flowers in many a
  crown,
Where all is rest and mirth, where wood-nymphs
  play,
And Pan still pipes beneath the friendly shade.

ASHLEY HORACE THORNDIKE.

TO A FRIEND IN LOVE

In Arcady ! I envy you.
Arcadian hillsides never knew
   A more bewitching shepherdess
   To take an humble swain's caress ;
Ne'er thrilled a shepherd heart more true.

Has not each flower a magic hue ?
Has not the sky a richer blue ?
   Is not life sweet — come, now confess, —
      In Arcady ?

With Pipe and Book

One time I dwelt where now you do,
Old friend; — but loves that last are few —
   Now since I know your happiness,
   I'll try my luck again, I guess,
For I should like to be there, too,
            In Arcady.

                    LOUIS JONES MAGEE.

MY PIPE

Two years old, this little fellow,
Yet he's strong and sweet and mellow.
Yesterday, to-day, to-morrow,
Always sharing joy and sorrow,
Sticking by me like a brother,
Soothing far more than a mother.
      Two years old, and yet quite ripe —
      My little bulldog, brier pipe.

Yes, he goes to church on Sunday
(Oftentimes to worse on Monday);
Then, of course, he's under cover,
Yet this patient little lover,

A Collection of College Verse

Grumbling, hateful ways disdaining,
Ne'er was known to be complaining.
    Two years old, yet strong and ripe —
    My little bulldog, brier pipe.

Over there at Charlie's soaking,
Round a social table smoking,
Pouring over analytics,
Talking football with the critics,
Making love to German lasses,
Walking 'midst the crowded masses,
    He is with me strong and ripe,
    My little bulldog, brier pipe.

Cheer and comfort always lending
With his curling smoke ascending;
Never cold and apathetic,
Always warm and sympathetic,
He and I are single-hearted,
He and I have never parted.
    Yes, I love this strong, this ripe,
    This little bulldog, brier pipe.

F. S. CAMP.

With Pipe and Book

RING-DOVES AND ROSES

O YOUTH and Love and plighted faith,
They laugh to scorn the thoughts of death
    With merry quips and dulces;
While memories of eyes of brown
And lids Maid Modesty kissed down,
    Beat softly in the pulses.

    And oh! and aye!
    As Time flies by,
    The sweetest chords may twang awry,
    And song oft sinks to sobbing.

But roses die in cheeks so fair,
White age steals lightly through the hair,
    The scorn of youth defying.
And compliment is out of tune,
And through the balmy bowers of June
    The Autumn winds go sighing.

    And oh! and aye!
    But Youth flits by,
    I catch the echo of a sigh
    Within my heart low throbbing.

    CHAUNCEY WETMORE WELLS.

A Collection of College Verse

OH, FOR THE STORM-SCARRED HEADLANDS

Oh, for the storm-scarred headlands,
   The hoarse, unresting seas,
The shifting mist and sunshine,
   The cool, soft eastern breeze!

Oh, to trace the low pine woodlands,
   Or walk the windy shore,
Or feel the muscle tighten
   Against the straining oar!

Sweeter than harp or sackbut
   To weary ear and brain,
The lapwing's low, wild whistle,
   The sea-gull's angry skane.

Better than books or study
   On gorse-grown cliffs to lie,
And watch the cloud-wrack slowly
   Climb up the summer sky.

Oh, for the blackened headlands,
   The hoarse, tumultuous seas,
The trailing mists and shadows,
   The strong, salt eastern breeze.

                A. M. LORD.

AT SWEET SIXTEEN

At sweet sixteen, with roseate hue
The blushing morn comes into view,
   And kisses with surpassing grace
     The beauty of a maiden's face.
O blushing morn, would I were you!

The maiden smiles, with love-light true.
Oh, would that love were *entre nous*,
   And in her heart I had a place,
     At sweet sixteen.

If she but felt, if she but knew,
The love which thus her beauty drew,
   Then, smiling o'er her happy face,
     I'd never leave the morn a place
To touch those lips, where Cupid flew,
     At sweet sixteen.

N. H. PITMAN.

APRIL

April, a lovely little maid thou art,
  Thyself so trustful and so pure in heart,
Thine hair of gold for dancing sunbeams meet,
  Thine eyes of blue and face so dainty sweet.

A Collection of College Verse

Alas, thine eyes are often filled with tears
   At eve, to gently sob thyself to sleep,
Next morn to wake, a happy child that clears
   Away all cares and sorrows, howe'er deep.

Around thy head, a wreath of mayflowers twined,
   White and sweet pink, thine own cheeks rivalling,
Breathing new hope and life in balmy wind
   Thou comest, cheerful daughter of the spring.

Thou bringest joy and peace to all mankind,
   And all our hearts in love to thee dost bind.

                        JAMES DAWES WILLIAMS.

A HUMBLE ROMANCE

Her ways were rather frightened, and she wasn't much to see,
She wasn't good at small talk or quick at repartee,
Her gown was somewhat lacking in the proper cut and tone,

With Pipe and Book

And it wasn't difficult to see she'd made it all
  alone.
So the gay young men whose notice would have
  filled her with delight
Paid very small attention to the little girl in
  white.

He couldn't talk the theatre, for he hadn't time
  to go,
And, though he knew that hay was high and
  butter rather low,
He couldn't say the airy things that other men
  rehearse,
While his waltzing was so rusty that he didn't
  dare reverse.
The beauties whom he sighed for were most
  frigidly polite,
So perforce he came and sat beside the little
  girl in white.

She soon forgot her envy of the glittering *beau
  monde*,
For their common love of horses proved a sym-
  pathetic bond.
She told him all about the farm, and how she
  came to town,

And showed the honest little heart beneath the
  home-made gown.
A humble tale, you say,—and yet he blesses
  now the night
When first he came and sat beside the little girl
  in white.

JULIET WILBUR TOMPKINS.

IF I BUT KNEW

If I but knew what the tree-tops say,
  Whispering secrets night and day;
If I but knew what the birds on high
  So sweetly warble beneath Love's sky,
    I'd make a song
      For you
To sing throughout your whole life long —
    If I but knew.

If I but knew how the lilies brew
  Nectar rare from a drop of dew;
If I but knew what in trellised bowers
  The night-winds tell to listening flowers,
    I'd make a song
      For you,

With Pipe and Book

And speak of days when Love was strong —
        If I but knew.

If I but knew what brook and river
    Murmur softly, murmur ever;
If I but knew a tuneful word,
    Sweet as the note of a wooing bird,
        That word I'd sing
            To you,
An answer from your lips to bring —
        If I but knew.

DIE WEINSTUBE

The coziest nook
That good friends know
Is the little old room at the end of the hall,
Wherever you look
The maxims show,
And there in a row,
Good comrades all,
Hang seven old tankards on the wall.

A Collection of College Verse

  A good man laughs
  In a jovial way,
Knows never the strength of sorrowful thrall,
  And vows as he quaffs
  That a king might pay
  To dream one day
  Where the shadows fall
Of life and love and dear friends all.

  Sympathy, cheer,
  And a lyrical song
And that is the way content is found.
  Hopes that are dear,
  Hearts that are strong,
  Cares that belong
  Under the ground,
And that is the way the world goes round.

  Old friends who hear
  Have never a moan
For dear days perished and buried all;
  Youth's young cheer
  Comes following on,
  So we take down
  When the dead leaves fall,

With Pipe and Book

Take down for youth and dear friends all,
The seven old tankards on the wall.

ROBERT L. MUNGER.

DOROTHY

In happy times and merry whiles
This song might garland o'er with smiles
The new-born love that cradled lies
Within thine eyes:

When far-off wedding bells a-chime
   Are touched with magic wand,
And life is at the crescent time,
   And all is fairyland,
Then Song and Echo in my rhyme
   Go straying hand in hand.

But if thy heart is turned from me,
Then empty is my heart for thee,
And this sad lay is wandering through:

When lilting love-songs lose their grace,
   And jealousies arise,

A Collection of College Verse

And steals a mist across the face,
Where love a-gazing lies,
O then are sobs in Echo's voice,
And tears within her eyes.

CHAUNCEY WETMORE WELLS.

FAIRYLAND

Sith none that breatheth living aire does know
Where is that happie land of Faerie. — *Spenser.*

Fairyland, oh, Fairyland!
Show us the road to Fairyland.
We are weary of work and woe,
Along our pathway the briers grow,
And high is the hedge on either hand,
Far have we fared from the Fairyland.
Fairyland, oh, Fairyland!
Show us the road to Fairyland.

Fairyland, oh, Fairyland!
Lost is the road to Fairyland;
Across the storied years it winds,
Through human hearts and human minds.

With Pipe and Book

None liveth now who may understand
The mystic magic of Fairyland.
    Fairyland, oh, Fairyland!
Lost is the road to Fairyland.

    Fairyland, oh, Fairyland!
Who will win back to Fairyland?
He who dwells in the yesterdays
May find the path o'er "ferny braes,"
May meet the queen of the elfin band,
And come to the long-lost Fairyland.
    Fairyland, oh, Fairyland!
Who will win back to Fairyland?

MARY HOLLANDS McLEAN.

TRIOLET

She wears a rose upon her breast;
    My heart is folded in the leaves.
By fine and filmy lace caressed
She wears a rose upon her breast,
And little dreams how fair a nest
    For my poor heart each petal weaves.
She wears a rose upon her breast;
    My heart is folded in the leaves.

IN THE DARK

HAVE you ever been a-walking on the grim old
  hills at night,
When the stars go twinkle-twinkle, and the
  moon is not in sight,
And the big trees in the forest seem to keep
  out all the light?

You hear a noise behind you, and you start, you
  don't know why,
And somethin' in the darkness seems to moan
  and pass you by,
And the blackness, gettin' blacker, shuts you off
  from all the sky.

Our ancestors were foolish to believe in spright
  or fay,
Or in ghosts that love the darkest night and
  always shun the day,
And that spirits of the dead still walk in their
  mysterious way.
Yet, though it's kind o' childish, I sometimes
  feel as though

They weren't so wrong as we believe, and
    maybe here below
There's more around us in the dark than any of
    us know.
JAMES BISSETT PRATT.

CHIVALRY

From out the deep and soulless gloom,
That his own hand could scarce relume,
A voice was heard, as from a tomb, —
    "For God and her!"

And straightway in that darksome time,
The kloster bells began to chime
In sweet, rare tones of song sublime, —
    "For God and her!"

Athwart the gloom bright arms flashed light,
While on the lance he bore, each knight
Inscribed these magic words of might, —
    "For God and her!"

Then ghastly shadows fled away,
And through the darkness stole the gray
Of hope's fair morning, and the day
    For God and her.

And when at last within its tomb
The knight had swept the lingering gloom,
Achilles-like, he faced his doom,
    For God and her.

The knight is gone; but yet we see
Within best manhood, beating free,
The ancient heart of Chivalry, —
    "For God and her!"

T. W. BUCHANAN.

TWILIGHT SONG

SWEETHEART, night is falling,
    Falling
Soft o'er land and sea,
And my love is calling,
    Calling
Through the night to thee.

Fairy fire-lights gleaming,
    Gleaming,
Dancing merrily,
Heed me not a-dreaming,
    Dreaming
Dearest heart of thee.

With Pipe and Book

But the shadows playing,
    Playing,
  Seek to comfort me,
And afar go straying,
    Straying,
Through the night to thee;

Till about thee bending,
    Bending,
  Tell with kisses light
That to thee I'm sending,
    Sending
All my love to-night.

THE NINETEENTH CENTURY

As one who, coming from a darkened place
Into full daylight, dazzled by the glare,
Sees nothing of the beauty that is there,
But only lurid spots that whirl and race;
And stands a moment with bewildered face
Till the mists vanish, and the landscape fair
Appears in all its glorious splendor rare
Where sun and wavering shadow interlace;

So we from ignorance, into the day
Of knowledge coming suddenly, assailed
By the fierce light of new-found truth, have failed
To see the glory that before us lay.
But presently the mists will clear away,
And, wondering, we shall see God's face, unveiled.

HARRY RUTGERS CONGER.

MABEL

When Mabel, in the springtime,
    Leans on the garden gate,
The blossoms come to meet her —
    The roses dare not wait.

When Mabel, in the summer,
    Stands in the grassy lane,
The daisies nod about her —
    Bees follow in her train.

When Mabel, in the autumn,
    Walks on the windy street,
The blushing leaves attend her,
    And chase her hurrying feet.

With Pipe and Book

When Mabel, in the winter,
  Rides in the merry air,
The snowflakes crowd to kiss her,
  And loiter in her hair.

While I, in all the seasons,
  Join the constant chase —
In turn, as flower or snowflake,
  Pursuing one fair face!

THE GLEE CLUB CONCERT

I

The club sings to-night —
  Are they nervous, I wonder,
Hoping all will go right
When the club sings to-night?
God save the poor wight
  Who by chance makes a blunder!
The club sings to-night —
  Are they nervous, I wonder?

II

My heart sings to-night,
  For to-night I will meet her.

Oh, the world is all bright,
And my heart sings to-night.
The club is all right,
  But I think my song sweeter,
For my heart sings, "To-night,
  Oh, to-night, I will meet her!"

III

The world sings to-night,
  Though the concert is over,
Oh, my heart is light!
The whole world sings to-night.
She has said that I might
  For eternity love her,
And the world sings to-night,
  Though the concert is over.

JAMES WEBER LINN.

FREE LANCES

A-RIDING, a-riding i' the growing morning light!
The bugles blow, and all a-row our lances glitter bright.

With Pipe and Book

Along the winding river, beside the beached sea,
By lonely tower, or high-walled town, or
    heathy wastes of lea;
Where'er we go, whate'er good cause our
    strong right arms may claim,
God guide us, merry gentlemen, and keep our
    swords from shame.

We squire to no lady's whims, we serve nor
    church nor lords,
But worship upon God's green hills, and love
    our own bright swords.
Let friars pray, and striplings love, and courtiers
    bend the knee,
While blood is hot and muscle firm, our hearts
    and hands are free.
A-riding, a-riding, — the east is all aflame:
God guide us, merry gentlemen, and keep our
    swords from shame.

                          AUGUSTUS M. LORD.

A RONDEAU

CLARISSA laughs. I plead in vain;
She hears my suit with sweet disdain.

When I remind her — speaking low —
That once she did not flout me so,
She asks me — do I think 'twill rain.
Then when in anger I am fain
To leave her, swear I've naught to gain
By staying, save th' increase of woe,
Clarissa laughs.

Yet when I beg of her to deign
To answer, give it joy or pain,
She smiles.   So then I cannot go,
For with her smiles my love doth grow.
Yet when I press my suit again,
Clarissa laughs.

RUTH PARSONS MILNE

A MISUNDERSTANDING

Came the West Wind, careless rover,
  Came and lightly kissed the rose.
    No one knows,
No one knows the whole world over,
  Why she turned her head away;

With Pipe and Book

Turned, his coming would not greet,
When the West Wind kissed her sweet.

Then the West Wind, reckless lover,
  Lightly, lightly shook the rose.
      No one knows
How, dismayed, he sighed above her;
  For her petals, one by one,
Fell, down-dropping strewn they lay;
Then the West Wind stole away.

S. C. W.

LOVE'S ORIGIN

MIDST the deepening shades of night, infant night,
  Look above, look above!
While the leaf a love-lay breathes from its height;
While the shadows hide the dross and the blight;
  All is love. All is love!
List the chant of distant bells on the air,
  Up above, up above!

A Collection of College Verse

Through the honey of the dew, O so fair!
Through the depth of silent thought, ah! up
    there
  All is love.   All is love!
Melting music from afar on the ears,
    God above, God above!
Lulls to sleep the rolling years, anguished
    years,
All the pain and bitter strife, inward tears,
  For all is love.   All is love!

ARTHUR D. CALL.

THE CROCUSES

HIGH in the night hung the moon, so cold,
Bending down to the earth, so old,
With her finger-tips on her icy lips,
Hiding her face in a cloud eclipse,
Silently touched the crocus cups,
  The shivering crocus cups.

Back shrank the spirit of Spring, so chilled;
Eyes with the tears of a hurt so filled;

But pitiful Night, with a coverlet white,
Crooning a lullaby, tucked out of sight
    The quivering crocus cups.

Deep in the crocus heart, so still,
Slumbered the soul of Spring, until
Through the tears and sighs of April skies
The sun dropped a kiss on the wide, sweet eyes
Smiling up from the crocus cups,
    The trembling crocus cups.

MARY HEFFERAN.

POLLY, MY SWEETHEART

O, POLLY, my sweetheart, so tender and true,
Alone in the gloaming I'm thinking of you,
And Polly, my sweetheart, my heart says to me,
Wherever she is, she is thinking of thee!

O, Polly, my sweetheart, so tender and true,
How long are the days till I'm married to you,
And, Polly, my sweetheart, my heart says to me,
The days are as long, too, for her as for thee.

O, Polly, my sweetheart, so tender and true,
I'll laugh at the king when I'm married to you,
And, Polly, my sweetheart, my heart says to
    me,
She'll blush like the rose as she listens to thee.

O, Polly, my sweetheart, the dark day must
    come
When fond eyes are darkened and dear lips are
    dumb,
But, Polly, my sweetheart, my heart says to me,
Wherever the one is the other shall be !

S. A. JONES.

SONG

To-day's to-day, and what's to-morrow ?
Here's a tankard unto sorrow.
The past is dead, and who will borrow
    Care from what is yet to come ?
We have journeyed o'er the stubble,
Arm in arm with sad-eyed trouble,
Care will vanish as this bubble.
    Sing the louder ; are you dumb ?

With Pipe and Book

In this wine there lurks a fairy,
See, she bids you all be merry!
Drink a goblet of this sherry,
    Pledge with us again a toast!
Seize the moment e'er it passes,
Drink the wine up, drain the glasses,
Drink a health to all the lasses,
    Pledge the girl you love the most.

If the one that you adore is
Graced with all her wondrous glories,
Be she Bess or dark Dolores,
    You're the one to know it best.
And if other names incite you,
Here's to her who may delight you,
If in doubt this cup will right you,
    Pledge the one you last caressed!

In this draught you'll find a treasure,
Just but see its golden measure!
I will warrant there's no pleasure
    Such as lurks within this glass!
Let the outer world abuse us,
If they drank of this they'd choose us,

A Collection of College Verse

But in hollow love they lose us
  Till their dusty lives do pass.

EUGENE RICHARD WHITE.

MY OLD GUITAR

By some eastern river thy rosewood grew,
  Thy inlaid pearl in the restless sea;
What craftsman moulded thy bosom fair,
  Sounding with dreamy melody?

What maiden's fingers have swept thy strings,
  In the distant vistas of long ago?
What love-lorn gallant has sung his lay
  To thy tuneful cadence sweet and low?

What odors of romance round thee cling,
  As each chord swells in thy bosom deep?
Whispering long-forgotten loves,
  Trilling the soul to rest and sleep.

Oh, Muse, who dwells in the hollow shrine
  Of my old guitar with its tales of yore,
Grant me the power to wake thy strains
  In music sweeter than e'er before.

F. G. HINSDALE.

With Pipe and Book

JOCK AND JENNY

Oh, Jock and Jenny, they went to the fair;
So gay and so charming was never a pair,
No lad was so bold and no lassie so sweet, —
And the piper played faster to follow their feet.
    Trip it high!
    Trip it low!
Join hands and curtsey, then off with a swing,
And follow your partner around in the ring;
    Now fast!
    Now slow!
So long as the sun shines this bright summer
  day,
We'll trip it and skip it, so blithe and so gay.

Said Jock, "I've but threepence; 'twill be but
  a bite,
The parritch we'll sup on thegither the night."
Said Jenny, "'Twill do for a bit o' a treat;
Let's laugh and be merry, — there's nae need
  to greet.

"There's ane for a token; we'll break it in
  twa,
And swear to be leal till the last day o' a'";

A Collection of College Verse

And ane for a ribband to twist in my hair,
And there's ane for the piper and there's — naething mair."

Said Jock, "I'll not hunger; I have na a fear,
For I'll feed on the smiles o' your mouth, Jenny dear;
As for drinkin', the glent o' your bonnie brown ee
Is makin' me toisie, as 'twere barley-bree."

Then Jenny looked up with a roguish surprise,
And whispered, "Sure, Jock, ye are tellin' me lies;
But whilst ye are dinin' sae dainty and well
I'll be wantin' a bit o' a sweetie mysel'."

Oh, Jock and Jenny, they went to the fair,
So gay and so charming was never a pair,
No lad was so bold and no lassie so sweet, —
Going home in the moonlight thro' acres of wheat.

LOUIS PACKARD GILLESPIE.

With Pipe and Book

THE FIRST SNOWSTORM

A Child's Poem

Little Miss Snowflake, dressed in white,
Came down the dusty road one night.
Her dress was as white as a piece of chalk,
And she pranced around, but did not walk;
For she was going to a ball that night,
And that was the reason she dressed in white.
There were fifty thousand, and many more, too,
And they looked like the children that lived in
    the shoe.
They had for music, that happy night,
A little brook that sang about flight;
They had for chorus the rustling leaves
That came from the top of the tallest trees.

EMILY EUGENIA MORRIS.

UPON HER MANDOLIN

The roses climb and cluster
   On Margery's lattice tall;
Aloft, with lucent lustre,
   Stars gem the heavenly hall;

A Collection of College Verse

Soft cadences are straying
　　Where silence late hath been:
'Tis bonny Margery playing
　　Upon her mandolin.

The crickets cease their trilling
　　Amid the grassy aisles;
Charmed by the music thrilling,
　　The drooping jasmine smiles;
The mocking-bird, delaying,
　　Forgets his silvery din,
And lists to Margery's playing
　　Upon her mandolin.

In envy, 'neath her bower,
　　Whose blossoms scent the gale,
Her lover sees a flower
　　The slender lattice scale;
I ween there is no saying
　　What he'd not dare, to win
The brown-eyed Margery playing
　　Upon her mandolin.

　　　　　　　　　CLINTON SCOLLARD.

With Pipe and Book

SUPPOSE

A SOFT cloud is drifting away in the night, —
Drifting away in the pale starlight;
With the gentle moon to shine on me,
And the glimmer of stars for company,
Wrapped in the downy folds to lie,
With the night-wind to kiss me a soft lullaby,
Answer me, is there sweeter bliss
        Than this?

But what if the storm-winds should arise,
As I drift with the cloud thro' the starlit skies;
And the moon should hide and the stars go in,
And with tear-drops big should the rain begin,
I cannot but think that I might weep too,
As my soft downy quilt to a wet sheet grew;
And I might be dropped in a big thorn tree.
        Ah me!

THE SONG OF THE JOLLY FAT FRIAR

A JOLLY fat friar once lived in a dell;
He told oft his beads, and he toll'd oft his bell;

A Collection of College Verse

Though he didn't fear heaven, he wouldn't fear hell,
For he liked Billy Satan a trifle too well.
CHORUS:
*Oh! 'Twas ding! dong! ding! dong!
gluckety! gluckety! gluck!
He pulled at the bell, a good pull and strong,
Then pulled at the flagon for luck,
With a gluckety! gluckety! gluck!*

This jolly fat friar threw over his care,
With merry good fellows and jolly good fun.
He learned from the wine-cup a new-fashioned prayer,
And morning and evening he'd over it run.
CHORUS:
With a ding! dong! etc.

It 'gan with the famous old Latin word "hoc,"
And rambled along o'er the saints of his stock,
Till the flagon grew thin and his mutterings grew thick,
When it ended itself with an infamous "hic!"
CHORUS:
Oh! 'twas ding! dong! etc.

CLAY ARTHUR PIERCE.

With Pipe and Book

A VALENTINE

I'm penning you a greeting
   This sweet confession-time
With Cupid gently beating
   The music of its rhyme.
Pray list to my entreating,
   Pray read this pleading line,
For I in song so deeply long
   To be your Valentine.

My page will soon be bearing
   This message Love has framed,
And eager hopes preparing
   To share what it has claimed;
Let, dear, your heart be daring,
   Give Cupid but a sign
That he may say for this one day
   I am your Valentine.

My page will whisper sweeter
   Confessions than I write;
His cunning wings are fleeter
   Than flash of morning light.

A Collection of College Verse

> Forth, Cupid, then, and greet her,
>   Breathe magic words of thine,
> And backward fly, and say that I
>   May be her Valentine.
>
> S. T. LIVINGSTON.

WHEN LOVE WAS BORN

When Love was born, he found all nature
    drear;
The silent birds knew naught of friendly cheer,
    And forest trees were bare. The sweet
      breath'd pine
      Gasped on the earth. But nature 'came
        divine
When Cupid dropped from God with winged
    spear.

Each star, till then fast fixed in its sphere,
Sped through the shady blue like startled deer,
    And knelt adoring at some planet's shrine,
      When Love was born.

The birds built nests, rejoicing far and near;
The air was music with their glad career;

With Pipe and Book

Light zephyrs kissed the joining tree and vine:
For God gave to the world this Valentine,
And bade the sun-clouds drop a joyous tear,
    When Love was born.

NORMAN HUTCHINSON.

MY LADY NICOTINE

REALMED in the dreams of Fancy,
    Crowned with the pearl of smoke,
From the lost land of necromancy
    My lady of old I invoke
My lady of Nicotina,
    As gay as the laughter of dreams,
As subtle as purring waters,
    As fair as the woodland streams.

Crowned in moments of pleasure,
    A friend in time of fear,
Like the sway of a love-caught measure,
    She speaks her word in my ear,
Until in moments of longing
    She banishes doubt and regret,
And I touch her lips uplifted
    With the wand of my cigarette.

A Collection of College Verse

You awake from the dreams of Hashan,
  There is doubt in your castles of Spain,
Love lurks in eyes Caucasian
  To leave them again and again;
Yet soft at the hint of my bidding,
  There floats on my vision a queen
Who lurks in dreams and fancies,
  My lady of Nicotine.

THE NIGHT-WIND'S SONG

The night-wind sings ever of thee, sweetheart,
    Tenderly low;
The night-wind bears its song to me, sweetheart,
    Through moonbeams' glow.
And the night-wind's song and mine are one,
And together of thee we sing, my own,
    We love thee so.

The night-wind has drunk of thine eyes, sweetheart,
    And kissed thy hair.
The night-wind thy every glance espies, sweetheart,
    Thy joys doth share.

With Pipe and Book

And ever it brings a breath of thee
That fills my soul with ecstasy,
  Oh, sweetheart fair.

HARRY C. PORTER.

LULLABY

Dreamily, dreamily, swinging, swaying,
  Blow as the blossoms blow, —
Babekyn rocks in a faery cradle,
  Now high, now low.

Babekyn rocks in faery cradle,
  Hung from the white moon's horn,
Pillowed on clinging, shimmering fleeces,
  From bright clouds shorn.

Merrily, gleefully, tossing, rocking,
  Sunshine on every side,—
Appleblows daintiest, sweetest, palest,
  His Majesty hide.

Gleefully, daintily, swinging, swaying,
  Blossoms blow light in the wind;
Dawn-tinted petals fall thickly, till Baby
  Is hard to find.

A Collection of College Verse

Wearily, wearily, rocking, swaying,
   Even the robins rest;
When the sun is dead and the blossoms shiver
   Long dreams are best.
EMILY S. JOHNSON.

WHERE LOVE DWELLS

Canst thou tell me where love dwells?
Is it in the tender bells
   Of the wakening flowers at morn?
Is it in the starry skies,
Ever twinkling lullabies
   To the spirits sorrow-worn?

Canst thou tell me where love sleeps?
Is it in the mystic deeps
   Of poet's fondest fancy?
Poesy! the echo long
Of thy minstrelsy and song
   Dies as a music on the sea.

Where, then, tell me, dost love rest?
It is in the heart that best
   Bears its sorrow love is born.

With Pipe and Book

In gentle Faith — there love abides
Whispering that naught besides
Holds the spirits sorrow-worn.

LEWIS L. BRASTOW.

IMMER MEHR

It was just a sweet song that she sang,
  A mystic and wonderful song;
Through the halls of my being it rang,
  And echoed so clear and so strong
    That I cried, "This is more than a song."

It was only a word that she spoke,—
  A tender and beautiful word;
Yet the voice of my passion it woke,
  As dawn wakes the voice of a bird.
    And I said, "This is more than a word."

It was only a clasp of the hand,
  And a glance from two lovely dark eyes
That timidly, dreamfully scanned
  My own, seeking love to disguise,
    But I saw there was love in her eyes.

A Collection of College Verse

And the love half-concealed in her eyes
  Met the love that was restless in mine,
And her blushes were sudden to rise
  As the tongue of the flame by a shrine.
  Then I whispered, "I know she is mine."

                THOMAS POTTER SANBORN.

MY HOUNDS

When 'neath my window's bar my good hounds growl,
  And through the darkness frantic rushes make
  At unseen foes, until the echoes wake
And lift their voices up in answering howl;
Then do I scorn the terrors of the dark,
  And laugh aloud, and cry out in delight,
  "No danger need I tremble at to-night —
    My good hounds bark."

But when no deep-toned baying breaks the hush,
  When all the silent night my ears I strain
  To hear their watchful muttering, in vain,

With Pipe and Book

And the ground quakes not with their sudden rush,
Then shadowy forms my chamber seem to fill,
  And stealthy footsteps on the stair I hear;
  My heart leaps, quivering with a nameless fear —
    My hounds are still.

JULIET WILBUR TOMPKINS.

SONG OF RETURN

Come, love, come where lilies blow,
  For the long grass waves in the sun,
And the wind is kissing the dew from the flowers
    One by one.

Oh come where wandering rivers find
  Their home in the heart of the sea,
And I'll tell thee how this vagrant heart
    Hies back to thee.

Come o'er the hills to the Sunset Gate,
  When crimson couriers run

A Collection of College Verse

To tell in the land of the Evening Queen
    That Day is done.

Oh come to the glimmering lake's brown marge,
  Where the waters soon will be
At rest with the holy vesper hour;
    So I with thee.

Come out in the silent night, my love,
    Oh come to me!
For I am here beneath the stars,
    Returned to thee,
And thou art mine, I thine for all
    Eternity!

A. S. C.

PROM. ROSES

Only a bunch of roses fair,
  A cluster of pink and white,
Roses that nod to the music low,
  The flowers she wore that night.

She tenderly lifts each drooping head
  That gracefully tosses there,
And the dainty flowers, nestling close,
  Smile back at the maiden fair.

With Pipe and Book

"How beautiful they are," she said,
   As she pressed them to her cheek,
"Why, the opened petals almost seem
   As if they were trying to speak."

I wonder why she cannot hear
   The song that the flowers sing,
I wonder if she knows or cares
   For the message the roses bring.

JAMES P. SAWYER.

LOST LOVE

In my heart a silent chamber,
No one dwells there, no one enters.
From the walls the busy spiders drop and spin
    their webs of gauze,
Watch and weave in vain endeavor,
Weak and dying, fall forever,
While the gray dust sifts and settles, all along
    the barren floors.

Once it was the scene of splendor,
Light and gladness, joy and glory,
There my princess dwelt in beauty, never seen
    on earth before;

And the candles by the fire
Leaped and quivered with desire.
Joy that she should look upon them, longed to
    feel her presence more.

By the ancient carven portal
Hangs the key now rusted, broken,
And across the bare, garret windows stretch
    the curtains, old and thin;
Time has dimmed them, moths have eaten,
Winter storms have tossed and beaten.
In my chamber, silence, darkness; sunshine
    never enters in.

THE STAR OF BETHLEHEM

O<small>NE</small> star from all eternity has hung,
    The porch-light of God's house, to be a guide
    To weary angels, speeding to his side
From ministry on earth; and shines among
The lesser lights with glory that has sprung
    From nearness to his presence, and the wide
    White gates of Heaven, where the hosts abide
Who chant his praise with undefiléd tongue.

With Pipe and Book

But once, when wise men journeyed from afar
   With gifts of gold and incense in their hands,
God left the portals dark, and sent his star
   To guide their footsteps over desert sands,
To where, in stable, as the oxen are,
   A little child lay wrapped in swaddling bands.

ELIZABETH KEMPER ADAMS.

DREAM SONG

At eventide, at eventide,
   When the golden sun drops into the sea,
Then over the waters, deep and wide,
   The little dreams wander so gleefully.
Some come on rafts, and some in boats,
Or anything else that sails and floats!

They moor their ships, they moor their ships,
   Just as the stars begin to peep,
And silently each little dreamling slips
   Through the nursery windows, where children sleep.
And they sit on the children's pillows all night
Telling them stories till broad daylight!

They tell such tales, they tell such tales,
  Of gardens as fair as the Paradise!
Of mermaids and nixies, — and giant whales
  That live far north, midst the snow and ice, —
Or of countries where always 'tis Saturday,
And children do nothing else but play!

But when dawn draws nigh, when dawn draws nigh,
  The dreams flit back to their boats again,
And the stars, one by one, drop out of the sky,
  And the moon's bright lamp begins to wane.
Then they sail to the land of the rising sun
To wait there and play, till day is done.

GERTRUDE CRAVEN.

WHERE CUPID DWELLS

Way over the seas, in a far, far land,
  Where skies are blue and gold;
Where ripples break on a silver sand,
  And sunbeams ne'er grow old;
There's a dale where Cupid dwells, they say,
And 'tis there that he rests from his frolic play.

With Pipe and Book

Oh, there's many a lass and many a swain
   That knows of his shafts made there;
For Cupid spares naught of a deep heart-pain,
   Though love be all his care.
And I think he should make a reflection or two,
When he rests over there from his play. Don't
   you?

ROBERT L. MUNGER.

WOODLAND WHISPERS

O groves of my own dear home-land
   Wrapped in tender twilight shades,
My soul goes out in longing
   For your dim and sheltered glades,
With their sweet familiar murmurs
   Which I still in fancy hear
Like a strain of distant music,
   Falling soft upon my ear.

O dells of my boyhood roamings
   Glamoured with the spell of youth,
'Midst your soft and hallowed gloamings
   Every fancy seemed a truth,

A Collection of College Verse

And the pure untainted fragrance
    Breathed from out the forest aisles
Seems to haunt me in my vagrance
    Through the weary waste of miles.

Ye dear and hallowed echoes,
    With your wistful, sad refrain,
Ye breathe through all my spirit,
    Till I scarce can quell the pain
Of the longing for the dear days
    That have fled into the gloom,
With the dusky, tangled byways
    And the woodland's sweet perfume.

R. P. COOKE.

SONG OF THE SEA FLIGHT

Sing ho! sing ho! for the sailing, O!
For the salt, salt surge and the winds that blow!
And the foam that's flung from the rail, bent low
    O'er the roaring sea!
Sing ho! then, loud, for the rattling shroud,
The whistling gale, and the scudding cloud,
And the gay gull soaring on pinions proud
    So far and free!

With Pipe and Book

Sing ho for the stars that bloom at night!
For the streaming wake, soft-sown with light!
And the face that shines in the moon's mist
    white
        Near, near, and sweet!
For the tale oft-told that will ne'er grow old,
The shy, sweet glance, and the hand-clasp bold,
And the mad, wild music that young hearts hold
        When warm lips meet!

Then ho for the salt sea's breath divine!
It thrills the blood like the rage of wine
As, borne by long billows that shake and shine,
        We lose the lea!
Unsullied the breezes sing and sweep;
Forgot are dull shoreward hours that creep;
With joy past naming our pulses leap
        Far out at sea!

W. C. H.

A MAY SONG

Heydey! for the maids of May!
Love alone is the game to play!

Turn on me your girlish glances,
Every look my love enhances,
Every smile my heart entrances,
Oh, May, I pray but stay!

Heydey! for the maids of May!
Laughing, loving, blithe and gay!
Laugh and part your lips in singing,
Let my heart with echoes ringing,
Haste the hours upon their winging,
Oh, May, but stay, I pray!

Heydey! for the maids of May!
Love and life have come to stay!
Still, alas! whilst I am singing,
List how Cupid's bow is ringing,
See how deep his darts are stinging,
Oh, May, I pray, *away!*

CHARLES SUMNER PIKE.

JACQUEMINOT

ARE you filled with wonder, Jacqueminot,
Do you think me mad that I kiss you so?
If a rose could once of its thoughts express,
I'd find you mocking, I more than guess;

With Pipe and Book

And yet if you vow me a fond old fool,
Just think if your own sweet pulse was cool
When you lay in her tresses an hour ago,
            Jacqueminot.

This pale, proud girl, you must understand,
Held all my fate in her small white hand,
And when I asked her to be my bride,
She wanted a day to think,—decide;
And I asked her, if her answer were *no*, she'd wear
A Marshal Niel to the ball in her hair,
But if 'twere *yes*, she should tell me so
            By a Jacqueminot

My heart found heaven; I had seen my sign,
And after the dance I knew her mine.
And I plucked you out of her warm, soft hair,
As her stately pride stood trembling there,
And I felt in the dark for her lips to kiss,
And I pressed them close to my own like *this*,
And I held her cheek to my own cheek—*so*,
            Jacqueminot.

                FREDERIC LAWRENCE KNOWLES.

A Collection of College Verse

SONG

The dawn is where thou art,
   (*My own sweetheart!*)
In thee all songs and voices blend
In one sweet singing without end.

The stars are like thine eyes;
   (*In them love lies!*)
In their far depths I seem to see
Bright visions of eternity.

Dawn and the stars depart,
   (*Not thou, sweetheart!*)
But from my soul the dream of May
And thee, can never fade away!

HENRY HUNTER WELSH.

LETTING DOWN THE BARS

I

Twilight falls from out the sky,
   And the moor-hen, sad and lone,
Sobs aloft her dismal cry
   As I drive the cattle home.

With Pipe and Book

O'er the moor her voice is calling,
Sweet inflections, rising, falling,
   'Neath the promise of the stars,
And 'twixt moor and meadow lands,
By the rustic gateway stands
   Jessie, letting down the bars.

II

Fairy fancies faintly fall
   In the chambers of my brain,
And I seem to hear her call
   O'er the woodland hills again.
Through the noise, the toil, the strife,
All the cares of busy life;
   Through the prizes and the scars,
In my dreams I seem to see,
With her brown hair floating free,
   Jessie, letting down the bars.

III

Jessie kissed the Prince of Death,
   And he bade her silent lie;
But the sound of memory's breath
   In my heart can never die!

A Collection of College Verse

When I bring my flock of years,
Gilded hopes and faded fears,
   To the city in the stars,
I shall see my darling wait,
I shall see, within the gate,
   Jessie, letting down the bars.

ARTHUR HOBSON QUINN.

FAYRE LADYE LALAGE

Belowe her Ruffe twinne Rosebuddes showe, —
My Gifte to her; — in Accents lowe
   She blushed and rendered Thankes to mee
   With such sweete Grace and Courtesie
Y^t in my Hearte, Hope's Flower doth blowe.

Y^n wille I presse my Suit, altho'
I maye not guesse her Fancy's flowe
   Y^e Buddes nodde "Courage," certainlie,
      Belowe her Ruffe.

Y^e wanton, wooing Breezes blowe
Her warme, darke Tresses to and fro,
   And kisse her little Lippes; — Ah, she

With Pipe and Book

Will let me kisse them, it may bee : —
Yᵉ merrie Bloomes, theye don't saye "No,"
    Belowe her Ruffe.

            THOMAS PORTER SANBORN.

TO A SPRAY OF VIOLETS

Violets blooming beside the road,
  Like fallen pieces of yonder sky,
Pray tell me who trespassed in your abode,
  And gathered your blossoms in passing by?

When I saw you, your heads were a-droop
  with shame,
  And your petals were closed for jealousy,
As I whispered to you when first you came,
  The name of a maiden dear to me.

But baptized, you repent of that sinful mood,
  As you lean from my vase you are wondrous fair,
And with all the grace of your native wood
  You give me the smile that she gave you there.

            ROBERT PRIESTLEY HAYES.

A Collection of College Verse

IN CAP AND BELLS

In cap and bells the jester sung
At court of king, and gayly flung
  His sparkling jests at high and low,
  And made the merry laughter flow
While yet our toiling world was young.

But now, ah ! now, the songs that sprung
From lips of old, and blithely rung,
  Are heard no more as long ago
        In cap and bells.

Yet should I bring, who long have hung
O'er mirthful tales of those who clung
  To motly, but the faintest glow
  Of their swift-flashing wit, I know
Not all in vain my lyre is strung
        In cap and bells.

              CLINTON SCOLLARD.

With Pipe and Book

NOW AND THEN

I

O THE days, and O the dances
Of that olden,
Golden
Time.
Swords and lances,
Tender glances,
  Love and laughter, war and rhyme
Made the wide world all romances,
  Life a song, a wedding chime!

II

Ho, sad Sir, I match the present
With your dusty,
Rusty
Time!
Knight and peasant,
Cross and crescent,
  These have passed, but life's old chime
Brings the same, now sad, now pleasant —
  Tears, love, laughter, joy and crime!

A Collection of College Verse

IN MODERN TIMES

WEEPING, there came to Venus, where she sat
   'Mid fairy bowers, within her Cyprian seat,
Her rosy son, Cupid, the archer boy,
   And flung his sheath of arrows at her feet.

For many years, upon love's mischief bent,
   He'd roamed at will, and sent his well-aimed darts ;
But now some evil god had charmed mankind,
   For lo, his arrows failed to pierce their hearts.

Then Venus comforted and soothed him ; called
   For clever Vulcan, and his sorrows told.
And Vulcan, smiling, gathered up the shafts,
   And tipped each little fairy point with gold.

Now Cupid, glad again, goes thro' the land
   Upon love's mischief bent, with bow and dart ;
And where his arrows once could not avail,
   Now, tipped with gold, they pierce the hardest heart.

HELIOTROPE

Heliotrope of gracile mien,
You that ever sunward lean
   In the morning's gleam and glow,
   Or when weary toilers go
Homeward 'twixt the hedgerows green,

Prithee, tell me, have you seen
Blithesome, debonair Irene,
   Heard her sweet laugh overflow,
                    Heliotrope?

Answer, you whose eyes are keen,
Did she, like a timid queen,
   Bend to you and murmur low
   Secrets that I long to know,
By this rose-tree's leafy screen,
                    Heliotrope?

CLINTON SCOLLARD.

A Collection of College Verse

I DREAM OF THEE

Ah, love,
When the fleeting shadows rove
O'er the summer hills with the breeze at play,
And the cricket shrills in the grasses high,
And the rainbow wings of the dragon-fly
Weave their fairy rings where the tall flags sway,
I dream, my love, of thee.

Ah, love,
When the round moon sails above,
And the plaintive note of the whip-poor-will
Greets my gliding boat, and the elfin light
Of the glowworm's torch sheds its lustre white
On my dewy march, and the night grows still,
I dream, my love, of thee.

CARL CHAPEAU.

SWORD SONG

A soldier of Fortune I,
The whole wide world's my home.

With Pipe and Book

I own for master no lordly king,
But astride my gray with a glove to fling,
And my good brown blade with bitter sting
O'er many broad lands I roam.
No fair dame's colors I wear,
No bright eyes flash for me;
My mistress is keen and hard and cold,
But truer than women and truer than gold;
In the clang of fighting she's free and bold,
    My sword's my love!

The rattle of dice is sweet,
And a rollicking song brings cheer,
But the grinding ring of blade on blade,
When thrust is turned with stiff parade,
When the game of death is bravely played,
Falls sweetest on my ear.
You may talk of pouting lips,
Or the ruby of rare old wine,
But when mad and hot the battle fares,
When he who wins is he who dares,
Then bright's the red robe my mistress wears —
    My sword!   My love!

Oh, we lead a careless life,
This brave old blade and I.

A Collection of College Verse

With swagger and swing thro' the world we'll ride,
And we'll hold together whate'er betide,
And when all is done she'll rest at my side
As cold and stark I lie.
Now here's to a steady wrist,
And a thrust that's always true,
And a blade that does never a danger shun,
That is never sheathed till the work is done,
Till the fight is over and victory won —
    My sword!   My love!

HARRY K. WEBSTER.

WHEN THE TIDE IS LOW

THE waves reach lovingly out to the sands,
    When the tide is low;
Gentle the touch of their tremulous hands
    As they restlessly ebb and flow.
Full many a shell whose rainbow hue
    Is softened and toned by the ocean's blue,
Do they bring to the wanderer's raptured view,
    When the tide is low.

And the old, old mem'ries they beckon to me,
    When the tide is low,

With Pipe and Book

As my bark glides over the evening sea,
   And the winds of the haven blow;
But *one* sweet, fond voice from the clust'ring throng,
   Unvexed, unmoved by my sin and wrong,
Calls back to me like an angel's song,
   When the tide of life is low.

ELLSWORTH LEONARD.

SERENADE

Sleep thou, mine own, while perfumed sighs
Of night winds whisper lullabies,
While Nature's tears in dew-drops fall,
And darkness dim envelopes all.

Sleep thou, mine own, while rippling streams
Murmur sweet music in thy dreams,
Soft melodies of cadence rare,
Which faint and die upon the air.

Sleep thou, mine own, while on the wings
Of Love is borne the song of strings
Æolian. Laying at thy shrine
My heart of hearts, forever thine.

Then sleep, mine own, till sunny day
Kisses thine eyelids, with a ray
From rosy-fingered goddess, Morn,
Whose beauty can but thine adorn.

THEODORE HINMAN SIMMONS.

THE BALLADE OF A KISS

Hair like a mist in the sun,
   Eyes like the blue of the sky,
Mouth like a rosebud half blown,
   Curved for a laugh or a sigh —
Pouting, yet peeping to spy,
   If the fate-bearing daisy told true;
As I stood there, demurely, I — why,
   I kissed her, of course, — wouldn't you?

That new waltz of Strauss' had begun, —
   That waltz throbbing hard like a cry
Wrought of pleasure, and pain all in one, —
   And the dancers went lazily by,
As she gave me the daisy to try
   Whether Cupid said anything new;
Then she sighed — oh, so softly, — and — why,
   I kissed her, of course, — wouldn't you?

With Pipe and Book

Just a kiss — what's the harm that was done?
    Not a soul in the garden was nigh,
And, you know, what is found out by none
    Never happened — none need to deny.
Just a kiss snatched from lips that were shy
    As the blush that across her cheek flew,
And the red of the rose would out-vie —
    I kissed her, of course, — wouldn't you?

    L'envoi!
Pretty maid, now my ballade is done,
    You ask, what's the moral to you?
I haste to reply there is none —
    But — I kissed her — *of course* — wouldn't you?

A. B. HOUGHTON.

MY QUEST

OVER the meadow and over the hill,
    Over the heath and heather, -
I seek for the spot where the dawn-wind sleeps,
    And slips from its night-bound tether.

A Collection of College Verse

    Is it here?   Is it there?
    Pray tell me where
The morning zephyrs tarry,
    That I may find
    Where they crouch and hide,
And sip of the dew they carry.

Over the billow and over the wave,
   Over the vales and valleys,
I seek for the spot where the night-wind dreams,
   And rest from its twilight rallies.
    Is it here?   Is it there?
    Pray tell me where
The breath of night lies sleeping,
    That I may rest
    In its downy nest,
With its breath my eyelids steeping.

AT THE SEA

Sing to me, Anemone!
At the breaking of the sea,
At the sighing of the deep,
Sing me into endless sleep!

With Pipe and Book

I am weary, very weary,
Lonely is the land and dreary,
When the waves break o'er the lea,
Sing to me, Anemone!
      — Dreamily, so dreamily!

When the breakers rise and fall,
When the wild sea-voices call,
When the sky is dark and chill,
When the sea-bird's cry is still,
When the cold north wind is blowing
Over ocean's icy flowing,
Spirit voices call to me;
Sing to me, Anemone!
      — Drowsily, so drowsily!

Sing a song of wilder kind
To the whistling of the wind!
Cold I lie upon the sand,
Cold the waves lap on the strand.
I am weary, oh! so weary,
Lonely is the land and dreary,
Lay me, dying, by the sea!
Sing to me, Anemone!
      — Sleepily, so sleepily!

HENRY HUNTER WELSH.

A Collection of College Verse

CHRISTMAS MORNING

With flare of trumpet and roll of drum
Tho' never a stick have we,
   And never a horn save a dimpled hand —
   A roistering, rollicking, warlike band,
Right valorous soldiers three.

Our line of march through the parlor dim,
And out to the open hall,
   A step and a stamp and a fearless stride —
   And a paper-knife strapped to each valiant side,
Then way! we are heroes all.

Shall it be a charge on the rocking-chair?
Or a siege of the balustrade?
   Or a slow, strategical night-attack
   On the castle walls of the old hat-rack,
Or merely a dress-parade?

'Tis one I vow to the soldiers three,
Polly and Prue and I,
   With never a horn save a dimpled hand,
   We'll march all over this Downstairs Land

With Pipe and Book

Till the stars peep out in the sky,
And the moon says bed-time's nigh.

CHARLES EDWARD THOMAS.

TWILIGHT SONG

Blow, idle shore-wind, low
   Over the lea ;
Flow, languid river, slow
   Down to the sea.

Fly, careless swallow, high
   Over the rill ;
Die, evening echoes, die
   Under the hill.

Stray, drowsy cattle, stray
   Into the fold ;
Stay, linger, twilight gray,
   Over the wold.

Sleep o'er our senses creep,
   Peaceful and light ;
Sweep all our troubles deep
   Into the night.

ROBERT L. MUNGER.

A Collection of College Verse

LATE

Why doesn't she come? The lamps burning faintly
But deepen the dark in the old-fashioned room
Save where over the fire-place a face pure and saintly
Smiles down its own light through the wavering gloom.

Her grandmother once who in silvery satin
Swept down those same stairs demure and sedate,
Shook out her long train in the gleam of the firelight,
And smiled, too, at making her own lover wait.

ANNIE NYHAN SCRIBNER.

YESTERDAY

At dawn a white-sailed vessel touched the pier,
Laden with gold and jewels rare for me;

With Pipe and Book

All day she lay in port, but in the clear,
   Calm even, with her gems she put to sea.

And mingling with a fleet, with bitter tears
   I see her white sails glimmer far away,
Sailing across the sea of wasted years,
   And know my gems are lost fore'er and aye.

WILLIAM H. FIELD.

CHEER

When the world's awry, when the tide is out,
   And the heart is dull the while,
There's naught can dispel the care and doubt
   Like a girl's bright, fearless smile.

All the chilling mists of gloom and fear,
   In a hard life's storm and whirl,
Will vanish before the saucy cheer
   Of a sweet-faced, laughing girl.

There's new life in the air of her sunny smile,
   Parting lips over lines of pearl,
And contagious hope in the dancing eyes
   Of a blithesome, laughing girl.

A Collection of College Verse

Not snowflakes white, as they mantle down
   Soft and light o'er the scars of earth,
Can as gently cover a vexed heart's frown
   As the spell of her cheery mirth.

All the weaker thoughts of a wayward heart
   Are folded away like a sail at furl,
Or summoned to play the nobler part
   By the smile of a true, sweet girl.

                 GEORGE BROWNING McCLELLAN.

A SKATING SONG

THE sound of the bugle over the hill —
   Ho! lads, ho!
The twang of the bowstring, silvery shrill
   Across the waste of snow.

Then busk ye, all my merry men,
   And arm ye for the fight,
There's many a heart now whole I ken,
   Will helpless lie this night —

With Pipe and Book

For who can brave a maiden's glance,
   Or ward her dear device —
What time the moonbeams are a-dance
   Along the diamond ice?

The gallant rush as the squadrons wheel —
   Away! lads, away!
The rollicking call and the ring of steel —
   Ah! but the world is gay.

So, merry men, lay down your arms
   And quit a vanquished field,
For we are bound by stronger charms
   Than Baron Frost can wield.
The icy chains of doughty Jack
   Must vanish at a breath,
But these fond ties we wear, alack!
   Shall hold us to the death.

Dan Cupid's bow is never still —
   And like a bell
Sounds Love's light laughter over the hill —
   A sweet farewell.

DAVID POTTER.

A Collection of College Verse

THREE POINTS OF VIEW

I — *His Apostrophe*

If my hopes were as bright
　As your eyes, *ma belle*,
When I whispered "Good night!" —
If my hopes were *so* bright,
I'd forget prudence, quite,
　And the world — ah, well!
If my hopes were as bright
　As your eyes, *ma belle!*

II — *Her Soliloquy*

If he weren't a dunce,
　And a dear, — ah me!
He'd discover at once,
If he weren't a dunce,
That I'm not, for the nonce,
　Wholly fancy free.
If he weren't a dunce,
　And a dear, — ah me!

With Pipe and Book

III — *Cupid's Complaint*

What's the good of a heart
 When the eyes are blind?
Or when pride takes a part,
What's the good of a heart?
Tho' I've sent my last dart,
 Not a wound to bind!
What's the good of a heart,
 When the eyes are blind?

D. V. C.

WHEN STARS COME OUT

When stars come out o'er land and sea,
And night winds, rushing wild and free
 From some dark billow's snowy crest
 To that bright island in the west,
Which now enshrines the form of thee,

I would, dear heart, that I could be
A spirit of the air, and flee
 To thine all loving arms and rest,
 When stars come out.

A Collection of College Verse

Such dreams the bright stars wing to me,
Through all the dim infinity,
   From airy regions of the blest.
   And so, by thoughts of thee caressed,
I sleep to dream again of thee,
      When stars come out.

———◆———

MY LADY IN THE GARDEN

Out through the blossoms she's wandering slowly,
   Down in her pathway the apple-blooms fall,
With scent of the lilacs, the air is made holy
   For her who is blossom and queen of them all.

Cover your heads and hide in the grasses,
   Lilies that nod so stately and tall.
She gathers you up in her hands as she passes, —
   They are whiter than you; she is queen of you all.

Kneel ye, pink roses; she's found out the treasure

With Pipe and Book

Of all your sweet incense down here by the
    wall;
Close to her cheek, if that be her pleasure,—
    It is pinker than you; she is queen of you all.

We, like the birds in the maple-trees o'er her,
    Follow her footsteps, we come at her call.
Only with that which is pure we'll adore her,—
    She, the white blossom, the queen of us all.

WILLIAM BYRON FORBUSH.

MANOA

"A faire citye of great wealthe."

Ho, comrades, seize your rusting arms,
    Recall your old bravado,
And away to seek the richest town
    In the realms of El Dorado.

Its roofs are covered with golden tiles,
    Upraised on columns golden;
Of gold are the pavements of the streets,
    Of gold the ramparts olden.

A Collection of College Verse

There are golden idols in golden shrines,
    In golden temples dwelling;
And the people heap them with golden gifts,
    In number past all telling.

A golden plough, or a golden spade
    Is the tool of the poorest farmer;
And with golden swords do its soldiers fight,
    Arrayed in golden armor.

But a golden idol is weak before
    An honest Spaniard's *credo;*
And their weapons of gold will scarce abide
    Our sabres of Toledo.

Then scour once more your rusty arms,
    Recall your old bravado;
We'll sack and plunder the fairest town
    Of the realms of El Dorado.

                              WILLIAM HOLDEN EDDY.

With Pipe and Book

THE LITTLE BLIND BEGGAR

At the gate of the World where the travel flows,
    And the folk stream by full-tide,
A little blind Beggar sits in the sun
    And shoots afar and wide.

He fits the arrow and twangs the bow
    And low in his throat laughs he,
For well he knows he will hit his mark
    Though never a face he see.

And never his stock of arrows fails,
    For the pain of the wound is sweet,
And the stricken folk bring the arrows back
    To pile at the Beggar's feet.

And he fits the arrows and twangs the bow
    And laughs till his fingers shake,
For well he knows he can never miss
    But somewhere a heart must ache.

And they who are struck, they keep still tongue,
    But they carry the arrows back,
And they who are spared, they sound abroad
    The songs of the pain they lack.

But still or singing, and grave or gay,
  Through the gate of the World they go,
And the little blind Beggar sits in the sun
  And laughs as he lays them low.

J. D. DASKAM.

LINES

Praying my Lady be a Little Girl again

> *" Some day she will learn to know*
>   *Child-faith, as of old*
> *Learn to look within, and so*
>   *Find the gold."*

Lady, one who loves thee sends this prayer,
Knowing thee wise and good as thou art fair.

Soul of the lily, heart of rose, you awoke
  To find the world that seemed so fair, a cheat.
Dream again, lady, the world's hearts are of oak,
  But they will guard thee from the storm and sleet;
Hands that are rough and restless from the strife
Will win and keep a peace about thy life.

With Pipe and Book

Dream again, lady, turn thy gentle eyes
   Aside from the world's bitterness and grime;
God's glory reigns above the hills that rise
   Eastward and westward toward the walls of time.
Beauty blesses the valleys; a little the world is true;
And a kindlier age is ours than that which our fathers knew.

Lady, look kindly out on the strife, and be
   To those who struggle a hopeful guiding star,
Ruling right queenly, keeping thy heart's heart free
   Till that heart's master, resistless, comes from afar.
Listen my prayer, lady; be unafraid as of old,
   Frankly challenging life with a smile. And see!
Because *thou* art true, lady, thy servants have hearts of gold.

A Collection of College Verse

SLUMBER SONG

SLUMBER sweet thine eyelids greet,
  Marguerite;
May the angels watching o'er thee
Sing their softest dream songs for thee,
  Marguerite, Marguerite.
May the night winds soothing speak,
 As they blow, soft and low,
  To and fro
O'er thy blushing, dimpled cheek,
  Marguerite,
Whispering Love's old melody,
  Sweet, to thee,
Till the morning sunlight beaming
Gently woos thee from thy dreaming
  Back to me,
 Marguerite, my Marguerite.
ST. RIC.

A MIDSUMMER NIGHT'S DREAM

MOONBEAM meshes tangled lie
 On the grass tops, in the hollow,
Round and round the wood nymphs fly,

With Pipe and Book

    Chasing hard the satyrs follow.
"Catch us, catch us, if you can,"
    Laugh the wood nymphs in the hollow.
Shout the satyrs, "Follow! follow!"
    "Catch us!" — "Follow" — "if you can."

All about the bright moon weaves
    Mingled shadows, softly falling.
In and out among the leaves
    Dance the wood nymphs gayly calling.
"Catch us, catch us, if you can,"
    Laugh the wood nymphs in the hollow.
Shout the satyrs, "Follow! follow!"
    "Catch us!" — "Follow" — "if you can."

Lower, lower drops the moon,
    Oh, the witching summer weather!
Hark, the midnight hour! too soon
    Moonlight, fairies fly together.
"Catch us, catch us, if you can,"
    Laugh the wood nymphs in the hollow.
Shout the satyrs, "Follow! follow!"
    "Catch us!" — "Follow" — "if you can."

FLORA E. BILLAM.

A Collection of College Verse

"WHEN THE LAST LIGHT DIM AND STILL"

"When the last light dim and still
Trembles on the western hill,
    Margaret,
      Do you yet
Stand beside the mossy rill
Dreaming else or singing low,
As I saw you years ago?

When the shepherds homeward go,
Faring silently and slow,
    Margaret,
    Margaret,
Do you ever, ever know,
Any of the evening yearning
Or regret's relentless burning?

Harboring, harboring
Melancholies in the spring,
    We forget,
    Margaret,
Peace dead memories might bring,
Dear words whispered soft and low
In the very long ago."

ROBERT L. MUNGER.

With Pipe and Book

A SONG

This I learned from the birds,
    Dear heart,
And they told me in woodland words
    Apart —
And they told me true,
That all their singing the summer through
  Was of you, of you.

This I learned from the flowers,
    Dear heart,
In the dewy morning hours
    Apart —
And they sware it, too,
That all their sweetness the summer through
  Was for you, for you.

This I learned from the leaves,
    Dear heart,
On stilly, starry eves
    Apart —
Though their words were few,
That all their sighing the summer through
  Was for you, for you.

FRANCIS CHARLES McDONALD.

"CRUX FIDELIS"

High in the snowy pinnacle
  Tinkle the silvery convent bells;
The brown-robed monks come half awake
  In shivering silence from their cells.

The night-wind blows the powdered snow
  Across the naked, sandalled feet
That shuffle along the cloister-stones,
  Hollowed with time and glazed with sleet.

They creep from the snowy cold without
  Into the stony cold within;
The organ fills the minster walls
  With muffled tones, and Lauds begin.

One taper lights the lectern-book,
  Red gleam the clanking censer's coals,
Into the darkness of the nave
  The great hymn of the Passion rolls.

  "Crux fidelis, inter omnes
    Arbor una nobilis;
  Silva talem nulla profert
    Fronde, flore, germine,

With Pipe and Book

>   Dulce ferrum, dulce lignum,
>   Dulce pondus sustinent."

Up on the shrouded altar-rood
　　The Crucified hangs pale and dim ;
The organ peals for Holy Week,
　　The monks sing on the ancient hymn :

>   "Sola digna tu fuisti
>   　　Ferre mundi victimam ;
>   　　Atque portum praeparare,
>   　　Arca mundo naufrago,
>   　　Quam sacer cruor perunxit,
>   　　Fusus Agni corpore."

The church is dark, the censer cold,
　　Its fire to ashes burns away :
The monks steal softly through the night
　　To dream of heaven's eternal day.

JOHN S. P. TATLOCK.

CLOUDLAND

Over the hills, at the close of day,
　　Gazing with listless-seeming eyes,

Margery watches them sail away, —
  The sunlit clouds of the western skies.

Margery sighs with a vague regret,
  As slowly they fade from the gold to gray,
Till night has come, and the sun has set,
  And the clouds have drifted beyond the day.

What are you dreaming, my little maid?
  For yours are beautiful thoughts, I know;
What were the words that the wild wind said,
  And where, in the dark, did the cloud-ships
    go?

Come through the window and touch her hair,
  Wind of the vast and starry deep!
And tell her not of this old world's care,
  But kiss her softly, and let her sleep.

———◆———

THE OLD LOVE SONG

PLAY it slowly, sing it lowly,
  Old familiar tune!
Once it ran in dance and dimple,

With Pipe and Book

    Like a brook in June;
Now it sobs along the measures
    With a sound of tears;
Dear old voices echo through it,
    Vanished with the years.

Ripple, ripple goes the love song
    Till in slowing time,
Early sweetness grows completeness,
    Floods its every rhyme;
Who together learn the music
    Life and death unfold,
Know that love is but beginning
    Until love is old.

Play it slowly, it is holy
    As an evening hymn;
Morning gladness hushed to sadness
    Fills it to the brim.
Memories home within the music,
    Stealing through the bars;
Thoughts within its quiet spaces
    Rise and set like stars.

A Collection of College Verse

DI'S SMILE

Have you ever seen Di's smile?
    Oh, 'tis pretty!
It is very worth your while,
If you ever hap to meet her,
Not to miss the chance to greet her
In the park or on the street,
To enjoy the subject sweet,
    Of my ditty.

If it does not stir your heart,
    More's the pity.
If you've ever seen the ripple start,
Coy with cherried lips opposing, —
Pearly glimpses, too, disclosing,
On the rampage, dimples, blushes, —
What are you that scornful, hushes
    My wee ditty?

WILLIAM CLYDE FITCH.

A STOLEN GLANCE

I sing of the grace of a fleeting face
    And the charm of a hurried glance,

With Pipe and Book

Of a form so neat and a smile so sweet
   In the maze of the whirling dance.
I see her alone; then the vision has flown,
   And the music grows dreamy and low.
The gay flashing light is not half so bright,
   And my heart-beats are heavy and slow.
But my heart I conceal till once more do I feel
   The magical charm of her glance;
For she blushes so sweet as our eyes again meet
   In the maze of the whirling dance.

                JOHN CLINTON ANTHONY.

WHEN MORNING BREAKS

When morning breaks what fortune waits for me?
What ships shall rise from out the misty sea?
   What friends shall clasp my hand in fond farewell?
   What dream-wrought castles, as night's clouds dispel,
Shall raise their sun-kissed towers upon the lea?

To-night the moon-queen, shining wide and free,
To-night the shining breeze, the song and thee;

But time is brief. What cometh, who can tell,
        When morning breaks?

To-night, to-night, then happy let us be
To-night, to-night, life's shadowy cares shall flee!
  And though the dawn come in with chime or knell,
When night recalls its last bright sentinel
I shall, at least, have memories left to me,
        When morning breaks.

EDWARD A. RALEIGH.

THE TARDY-BUG MEN

Where were they going, those Tardy-Bug Men,
  As they trooped down the hill to the valley?
And what did they do, and what happened when
  They trooped down the hill to the valley?
They carried the shadows to darken the land,
And they called to the toilers on every hand
To cease for the passing of Tardy-Bug band,
  As they trooped on their way through the valley.

With Pipe and Book

What were they singing, those Tardy-Bug Men,
  As they crossed by the bridge and the ferry?
Singing so sweetly along through the glen
  As they crossed by the bridge and the ferry?
They sang of the land of the Lulla-bye tree
Where dreams are grown ripely for you and for
    me,
And they brought of the fruit for the peasantry
  Who dwelt by the bridge and the ferry.

Where did they go, those Tardy-Bug Men,
  When they marched through the town and
    the country?
And when will they come through the valley
    again
  With dreams for the town and the country?
After the sun they must steadily creep,
Bearing their message of slumber, to keep
Girdling the earth with a rainbow of sleep
  For the men of the town and the country.

Why did they come when the sun had sunk low
  And go trooping along through the valley?
Why did they come from the East and then go
  Westward along through the valley?

A Collection of College Verse

Their path is as straight as the path to the sun,
And their way is as long, for it never is done!
And the day that they follow is never begun —
  For they carry the night through the valley.

ALDEN J. BLETHEN, JR.

WHEN CHIME THE BELLS

WHEN chime bells at even-tide,
And, spreading o'er the country-side,
  The quiet shadows softly fall,
  Contentment comes to one and all,
And happiness spreads far and wide.

And lovers, sitting side by side,
In strong affection true and tried,
  Their sweetest memories recall
    When chime the bells.

Their thoughts through realms enchanted glide,
And seem on wings of love to ride
  Through Fairyland's celestial hall,
  Where from their souls earth's troubles fall,
    When chime the bells.

LOUIS V. WINTER.

With Pipe and Book

BANQUET SONG

Comrades, fill the banquet cup
   Brimming up!
Fill it full of love and laughter,
Claret lips and kisses after;
 Crown it with a maiden's smiles
 And the foam of magic wiles.
Drink it, drain it, clink your glasses,
For the love of loving lasses
   Ere it passes!

Fill again the banquet cup
   Brimming up!
Overflow it with the roses
Which her timid blush discloses.
 With her sparkling eyelight sift it
 Till it flavored is.   Then lift it.
Drink it, drain it, clink your glasses,
For the love of loving lasses
   Ere it passes!

Comrades, fill a parting cup
   Brimming up!
Flood it in your praise's zest
For the uninvited guest.

A Collection of College Verse

With the charms and graces fill it,
Touch the lips and heartward spill it.
Drink it, drink it, clink your glasses,
For the love of loving lasses
    Ere it passes!

          EDWIN OSGOOD GROVER.

FOOL'S BALLAD

KING Solomon were dunce though he
    A tenfold wisdom carried,
But Solomon a sage was he
    A thousand times well married;
For lads will woo and maids will wive,
    And laugh at melancholy,
And *two-and-two* is counted *five*,
    Good thanks to Mistress Folly.

    Lads, fill your glasses, aye,
    Laugh as life passes by,
    Mirrored in lassie's eye,
    Here's to a fool.

There be of them though e'er so wise
    Whose clumsy feet go dancing,

With Pipe and Book

And follow after laughing eyes
   O'er dainty shoulder glancing;
But ah, such wisdom's in the braids
   Of pretty Peg and Polly,
I do but wanton with the maids,
   And woo sweet Mistress Folly.

Lads, fill your glasses, aye,
Laugh as life passes by,
  Mirrored in lassie's eye,
  Here's to a fool.

CHAUNCEY WETMORE WELLS.

DORIS'S SHOESTRINGS

On Doris's feet
   Are the smallest of twos;
But surely some elf
   Has enchanted her shoes,
For wherever we go,
   If we walk, row or ride,
In church or at tennis,
   Her shoe comes untied.

A Collection of College Verse

At times it is trying,
  But what can I do
When poor Doris murmurs,
  "Oh, bother that shoe!"
So down I must flop
  In the dust and the dirt
To tie up the shoe
  Of that dear little flirt.

These precious girl-tyrants!
  We cannot rebel,
For even their ribbons
  Are filled with their spell.
Since old-fashioned aprons
  No longer they use,
They tie a poor man
  To the strings of their shoes.

JULIET WILBUR TOMPKINS.

HER LIGHT GUITAR

Her light guitar she sweetly plays
With the sweetest, witching little ways
  Of smiling at me, as I lie
  Admiring her, and vainly try
To still the heart her beauty sways.
Her graceful form the fire's red rays
Encircle with a maddening maze
  Of mellow light,—and richly dye
    Her light guitar.

SOUTHERN

Out of my window, half dreaming, I leaned,
My hands full of passion-flowers carelessly
  gleaned;
  The night like some dusk damask-rose just
    a-bloom,
  All tremulous with its wealth of perfume,—
Yet sweeter than all the sweet night touched
  with dew
Was the thought in my soul of you, sweetheart,
  of you.

A Collection of College Verse

A silver-strewn main was the sweep of the sky,
Where the stars — timid sailors — thick-clustering lie;
   And far in the east a golden-lined boat
   Swinging wide at her anchor — the young moon afloat;
Yet fairer than all the night's beauty in view
Was the dream that it brought of you, sweetheart, of you.

From the south through the limes came a passionate breath
That the faint wind scarce bore ere it swooned to its death;
   Yet I grasped the sweet meaning with which it was fraught,
   And night, sky and stars — yea, the whole world — were naught
When once the full import my longing soul knew,
For a whisper it brought of you, sweetheart, of you.

E. M. LEVIER.

With Pipe and Book

TO THE VALLEY OF DREAMS

To memory-land we often go,
And yet, I wonder if we know
   Just why we slip from life's rough way
   To wander back for hours to play
'Mid other scenes that charm us so;

Or why, when sinking sun is low
And changing blue is all aglow,
We journey through the twilight day
      To memory-land?

But long as sunset breezes blow,
And field-flowers sweet wave to and fro,
   So long will you and I obey
   The tender notes, th' entrancing lay
Of bard of dreams, and hie, I trow,
      To memory-land.

T. B. R.

AUTHOR INDEX

Adams, Elizabeth Kemper, 93
Anthony, John Clinton, 24, 139

Billam, Flora E., 131
Blethen, Alden J., 141
Brastow, Lewis Ladd, 87
Buchanan, T. W., 62

Call, Arthur D., 70
Camp, Frederick Stanley, 48
Chapeau, Carl, 109
Conger, Harry Rutgers, 64
Cooke, R. P., 96
Copeland, G. A., 40
Craven, Gertrude, 94

Daskam, J. D., 128
Dillman, Will, 41

Eddy, William Holden, 126

Field, William H., 20, 119
Fitch, William Clyde, 139
Forbush, William Byron, 129

Gillespie, Louis Packard, 76

Gillette, George W., 33
Grover, Edwin Osgood, 144

Hayes, Robert Priestley, 104
Hefferan, Mary, 71
Hinsdale, F. G., 75
Houghton, A. B., 103
Hutchinson, Norman, 83

Johnson, Emily S., 34, 86
Jones, Gertrude, 39
Jones, S. A., 72

Ketchum, Arthur, 13, 36
Knowles, Frederic Lawrence, 23, 31, 99

Leonard, Ellsworth, 111
Levier, E. M., 149
Linn, James Weber, 2, 66
Livingston, S. T., 82
Lord, Augustus M., 51, 67

McClellan, George Browning, 120
McDonald, Francis Charles, 134

Author Index

McKinney, Fanny L., 35
McLean, Mary Hollands, 60
Magee, Louis Jones, 47
Merrill, Charles E., Jr., 13
Milne, Ruth Parsons, 68
Morris, Emily Eugenia, 78
Munger, Robert L., 28, 56, 95, 118, 131

Pierce, Clay Arthur, 80
Pike, Charles Sumner, 14, 28
Pitman, N. H., 52
Porter, Harry C., 85
Potter, David, 19, 121
Pratt, James Binett, 61

Quinn, Arthur Hobson, 101

Raleigh, Edward A., 140
Reed, Amy Louise, 25
Reimer, Marie, 21

Sanborn, Thomas P., 88, 103
Sawyer, J. P., 91
Scollard, Clinton, 78, 105, 108

Scribner, Annie Nyhan, 119
Simmons, Theodore Hinman, 112
Stamon, Frank L., 45
Stone, Henry Morgan, 15

Tatlock, John S. P., 135
Thomas, Albert Ellsworth, 27
Thomas, Charles Edward, 117
Thorndike, Ashley Horace, 46
Tompkins, Juliet Wilbur, 18, 53, 89, 147
Townsend, H. H., 30

Webster, Henry K., 109
Wells, Chauncey Wetmore, 50, 145
Welsh, Henry Hunter, 101, 115
White, Eugene Richard, 73
Williams, James Dawes, 52
Winter, Louis V., 143

www.ingramcontent.com/pod-product-compliance
Lightning Source LLC
Chambersburg PA
CBHW030348170426
43202CB00010B/1291